ASSASSIN'S
CREED

ESCAPE ROOM
PUZZLE BOOK

Published in 2022 by Welbeck
An Imprint of Welbeck Non-Fiction Limited,
part of Welbeck Publishing Group.
Based in London and Sydney.
www.welbeckpublishing.com

A CIP catalogue record for this book is available from the British Library

ISBN 978-1- 80279-106-8

Project Editor: Ben McConnell
Design Manager/Cover Design: Russell Knowles
Project Designers: Amazing15
Production: Marion Storz

10 9 8 7 6 5 4 3 2 1

Printed in Dubai

ASSASSIN'S CREED®

ESCAPE ROOM PUZZLE BOOK

EXPLORE THE WORLD OF ASSASSIN'S CREED© IN AN ESCAPE-ROOM ADVENTURE

JAMES HAMER-MORTON

WELBECK

CONTENTS

Introduction.. 1

How to Use This Book..................................... 2

Prologue.. 4

Chapter One: The Animus.............................. 14

Chapter Two: Training................................... 42

Chapter Three: Following the Trail................ 64

Chapter Four: Deceiving the Assassins......... 84

Chapter Five: A Hidden Tomb 110

Chapter Six: Stopping the Cult 132

Hints

    Difficult.. 154

    Medium 164

    Easy.. 174

Solutions 184

Credits.. 216

INTRODUCTION

Dear Reader,

Welcome to Assassin's Creed – a world of murder, deception and stealth.

The Assassins have played an active part in shaping every era of human history from the decades that Cleopatra spent ruling over her subjects in Egypt to the genius of Leonardo da Vinci during the great Renaissance of Europe, the Assassins have been pulling the strings behind the scenes and they now need new recruits to add to their numbers as new threats beckon.

Who is their newest recruit? A very good question, Reader, and the answer is simple: you.

The Assassins need your help to ensure that the nefarious forces trying to topple the balance of good and evil throughout time are defeated forever.

As you travel through history trying to track down your true enemy, you will be tested repeatedly, and your mind will need to be as sharp as the blade concealed on your person to decipher the many clues that have been left dotted throughout history.

Your skills of deduction, lateral thinking and ability to connect seemingly disconnected facts and figures will come in useful as you navigate through thousands of generations to aid the Assassins on their quest.

Understand, though, that if you make a mistake during any of your trips through time, you might find yourself unable to return to the correct place of origin and the information you have collected could be incorrect, which will cause you and the Assassins to fail ...

HOW TO USE THIS BOOK

This book is, most likely, different to any other puzzle book you've encountered.

Most puzzle books are orderly affairs. Regular structuring. Clearly defined challenges. Compact – if difficult – challenges. In other words, they're safe. This is a very different beast. To get anywhere with *ASSASSIN'S CREED©ESCAPE ROOM PUZZLES*, you need to approach the book one section at a time.

Each section is a puzzle made up of interlocking pieces. Some sections hinge on knowledge you acquired earlier on, while others are entirely self-contained. Usually, a section takes up an entire chapter, except, well ... when it doesn't.

To help Joey, our plucky hero, through the trials inside this book, you'll often need to think outside the box. The way to approach a section is to read through it, letting Joey show you the things they consider to be of importance. You'll know when you come to the end of the section, because they'll always make it clear that you need to come up with an answer before they can proceed with a handy SOLVE TO PASS box.

 SOLVE TO PASS

Do not read on – the answer may be revealed on the next page!

FOR **DIFFICULT** HINTS, TURN TO PAGE **155**
FOR **MEDIUM** HINTS, TURN TO PAGE **165**
FOR **EASY** HINTS, TURN TO PAGE **175**
FOR **SOLUTIONS**, TURN TO PAGE **185**

Once you've read over the section, go back and look at it again.

On this second pass, you'll know what it is you need to end up with – whether it's a word, or a number of so many digits, or a certain pattern. The puzzles you have to solve in each section will stand out, but exactly how to combine them, or what order to start it, may be less obvious.

The text of the book will always guide your way, but Joey's hand may be quite subtle in places. It might be as clear as seeing that one puzzle will give you a set of colours as an answer, and another needs a set of colours to use as a start point. But the link could as easily be thematic, say a certain geological nature to a pair of problems. The puzzles in a section might lead firmly from one to the next, or they might each give you a small piece that can only be combined with its fellows at the very end. So each section is, at the same time, a set of puzzles, a collection of hints, and a carefully interlocking jigsaw. Look

for phrasings, or concepts, or other patterns that will guide you through its maze.

Each chapter has three tiers of hints: DIFFICULT, MEDIUM, EASY. The difficult hints are there to give you a bit of inspiration on how to approach each separate puzzle in the chapter. You can learn much from the puzzles alone. The medium hints should help if you're stuck, and are in need of a pointer. And the easy hints are there for when you're well and truly confused, and they signpost the way forward, although no puzzle in this book is truly easy, even with the hints.

One final note: some puzzles will need physical manipulation to solve. When you see the scissors icon and dotted lines, you're probably going to want to cut things out and turn them into 2D or 3D shapes.

Good luck!

PROLOGUE

I blinked for what seemed like a second, but in fact, I had slept for hours. I thought it was a combination of a late shift yesterday followed by an early shift today that had led to the indiscretion, but it was easy to fall asleep when monitoring the CCTV feed at the museum. A movement caught my eye. Was it interference from the feed or was someone actually there?

Perhaps the sudden movement had been the cause of my sudden awakening. It wasn't worth the risk to ignore it. I leaped to my feet and grabbed a large flashlight before sliding around the corner toward the area in question. The place was darker than I expected. It was now late evening and my fingers struggled to find some of the light switches on the way.

The hallway was empty, but didn't look quite right. Podiums dotted the walls, and one in particular called out to me. I approached it. The artefact it housed looked different somehow... It had been turned around, that was it. Leaning over the velvet rope, I went to move it, barely thinking about the consequences of touching it. In fact, all I was worried about was the consequence of my sleeping on the job.

The artefact was an intricately designed cube shape; far from perfect thanks to the attrition of time. I examined it from all sides while I held it.

Letters on each side stood out, embossed by some ancient technique that I was sure I would be in awe of if I had any idea what it was. I didn't know much about ancient civilizations, but there had to be some meaning in the different number of dots on each side.

! SOLVE TO PASS

I needed to put the letters in the correct order. Once I had the order, I knew I could proceed.

6

FOR **DIFFICULT** HINTS, TURN TO PAGE **155**
FOR **MEDIUM** HINTS, TURN TO PAGE **165**
FOR **EASY** HINTS, TURN TO PAGE **175**
FOR **SOLUTIONS**, TURN TO PAGE **185**

"Open me," I uttered, touching the letters in order.

Suddenly, the centre of the cube began to give way slightly, much to my horror. Had I broken it?

My initial fear was replaced with wonder as the two halves began to rotate like some kind of three-dimensional puzzle cube. Spinning it seemed to do nothing. It wasn't loosening or unscrewing, but turning. I lifted it up and looked at what I believed was the underside to see a crevice, well hidden when it was closed. I inserted my fingers to find out if there was anything inside, and instantly felt the smooth coldness of metal. It was a blade – and a sharp one at that. Fortunately, it

didn't cut me but it did make me flinch, which caused the blade to dislodge from the cube and clang noisily to the floor. I picked it up and examined it, my mouth open in wonder.

"What are you, and why were you in there?"

A metallic sound rang in my ears as I brought the blade closer to my face. The ringing suddenly subsided, almost whooshing past me, like a sword rushing past my head. That was an odd metaphor... why did that come into my mind?

I automatically turned to follow the sound, blade still in hand, heading into another area of the museum entirely. I knew the museum well, but I didn't consciously think of where I

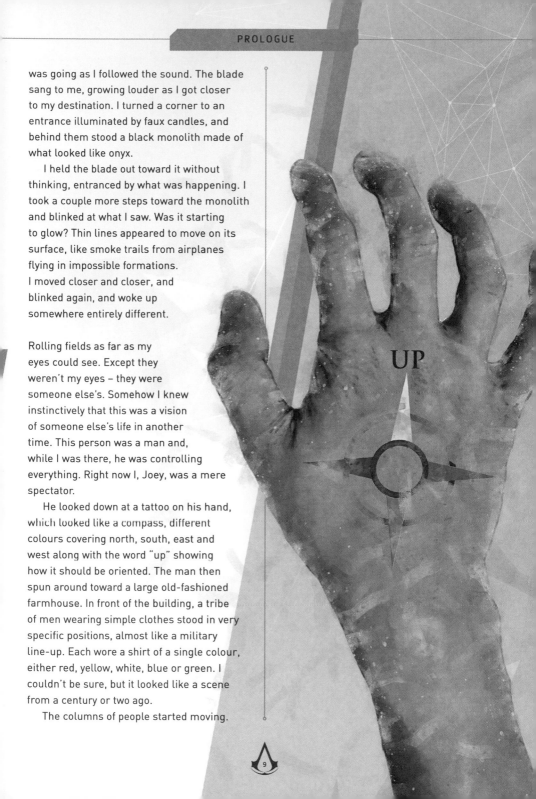

was going as I followed the sound. The blade sang to me, growing louder as I got closer to my destination. I turned a corner to an entrance illuminated by faux candles, and behind them stood a black monolith made of what looked like onyx.

I held the blade out toward it without thinking, entranced by what was happening. I took a couple more steps toward the monolith and blinked at what I saw. Was it starting to glow? Thin lines appeared to move on its surface, like smoke trails from airplanes flying in impossible formations. I moved closer and closer, and blinked again, and woke up somewhere entirely different.

Rolling fields as far as my eyes could see. Except they weren't my eyes – they were someone else's. Somehow I knew instinctively that this was a vision of someone else's life in another time. This person was a man and, while I was there, he was controlling everything. Right now I, Joey, was a mere spectator.

He looked down at a tattoo on his hand, which looked like a compass, different colours covering north, south, east and west along with the word "up" showing how it should be oriented. The man then spun around toward a large old-fashioned farmhouse. In front of the building, a tribe of men wearing simple clothes stood in very specific positions, almost like a military line-up. Each wore a shirt of a single colour, either red, yellow, white, blue or green. I couldn't be sure, but it looked like a scene from a century or two ago.

The columns of people started moving.

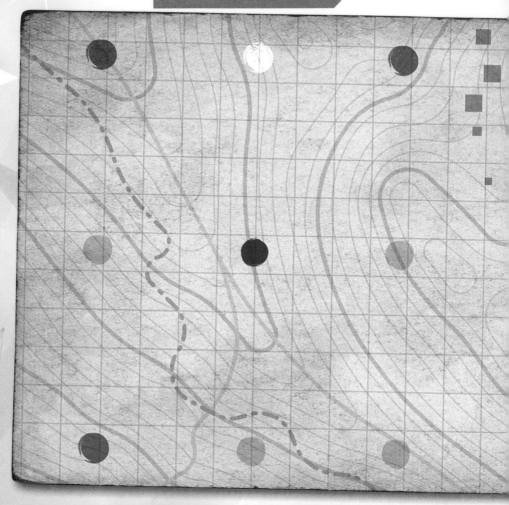

Those wearing white were stationary, while the ones wearing coloured clothes began pointing in different directions. It was quite bizarre, like an inexplicably rehearsed performance for my benefit. But was it for me, or the man I was part of? And was this actually something that happened, or a vision of some sort? For some reason, it all felt as if it was something real that had happened, as well as something important that I needed to see. Suddenly, I realized what was transpiring. A map of the tribespeople and their locations took shape in my mind, and I began to figure out the name of the man I was inhabiting.

SOLVE TO PASS

Once I knew the name of the man I was to find, I knew that I could proceed.

FOR **DIFFICULT** HINTS, TURN TO PAGE **155**
FOR **MEDIUM** HINTS, TURN TO PAGE **165**
FOR **EASY** HINTS, TURN TO PAGE **175**
FOR **SOLUTIONS**, TURN TO PAGE **185**

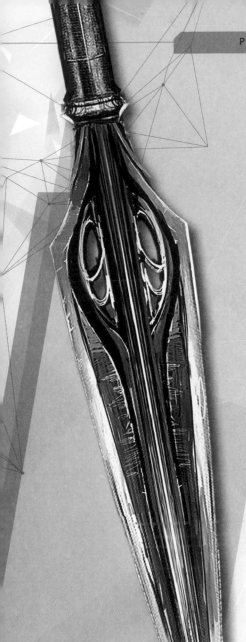

Sam. His name was Sam.

"Sam," called another man.

Sam turned to face the man with the gentle voice and the well-kept beard.

"Malcolm? I wasn't expecting you," he said nervously.

"Hush, my child. You have no need to fear me."

Sam nodded tentatively, clearly not believing the words coming from Malcolm's mouth. He looked down to see the bearded man brandishing a weapon, almost innocently.

I instantly recognized it. Well, half of it. This double-bladed dagger had its grip in the centre, and I was sure that I was in possession of one half of it. When did it get broken in two?

Malcolm gently raised the dagger a fraction of an inch, and the whole tribe – including Sam – fell to their knees, as if unable to resist some unseen power emanating from the blade itself. Sam could not even look up.

"Malcolm, please."

"Do you repent your sins, Sam?"

"I don't know what I've done."

Sam managed to flick his eyes up to look at Malcolm, but almost instantly, his gaze returned to the ground in front of him. In the flash of Malcolm I was granted, I suddenly realized from the shiny watch on Malcolm's wrist that this could not be a vision of the past. I had never seen a watch like that before. Was this a vision of... the future?

Malcolm raised the dagger toward Sam. It was impeccably clean and shiny, giving me a chance to finally glimpse the face of the man that I was inhabiting. A kind face, I thought. One full of knowledge – and, currently, fear.

"I knew this day would come," Sam announced, bravely.

"Then you know what must be done."

Malcolm raised the dagger into the air and

started appealing to his flock.

"My children, what do we do with traitors?"

The crowd shouted in unison, "Kill him!"

"You heard them," he said with a smug grin.

Sam struggled to raise his head to look up at the dagger. Then, just as Malcolm began to swing it toward him, I was shaken out of the vision by an explosion that rocked the museum. It felt like it had come from the direction of the cube.

"What was that?" I muttered, trying to assemble my already jumbled senses.

Voices started echoing down the corridors, and I was sure I heard somewhere among them the words "Joey, Joey..." and "blade".

I had to hide.

Without hesitating another second, I launched myself down the hallway in the opposite direction to the explosion, but the way

was already blocked by a menacing-looking figure wearing all black and brandishing a large assault rifle. A mercenary? I didn't wait to find out. My eyes widened in shock, and I scrambled back the way I had originally come, before veering off down the nearest alternate corridor.

As soon as I'd made the decision, I regretted it, knowing all too well that this led to a dead end. My only option was to hide. My mind leaped from cliché to cliché: an empty sarcophagus or large trunk would do, but nothing presented itself. There was a tapestry hanging just in front of the wall, which would do as a last resort, but it didn't reach the floor so it would still leave part of my legs exposed. But there was no other option.

"We know you have it," announced a voice, far closer than I was expecting.

"Down this way," another blurted out.

Then there was silence. I held my breath, but knew it was futile. In a few seconds, I would have to breathe out, and that would definitely give me away, assuming my exposed legs didn't do that first. All too quickly, footsteps broke the quiet and I knew it was only a matter of time before the mercenaries found what they were looking for.

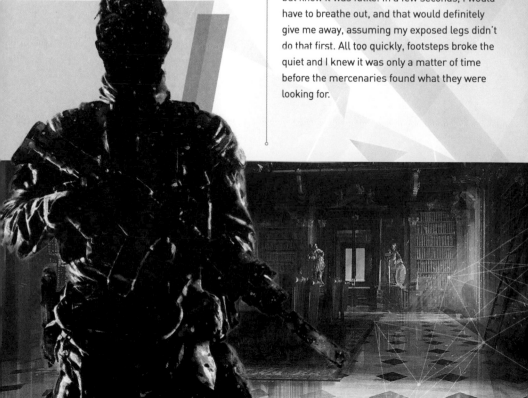

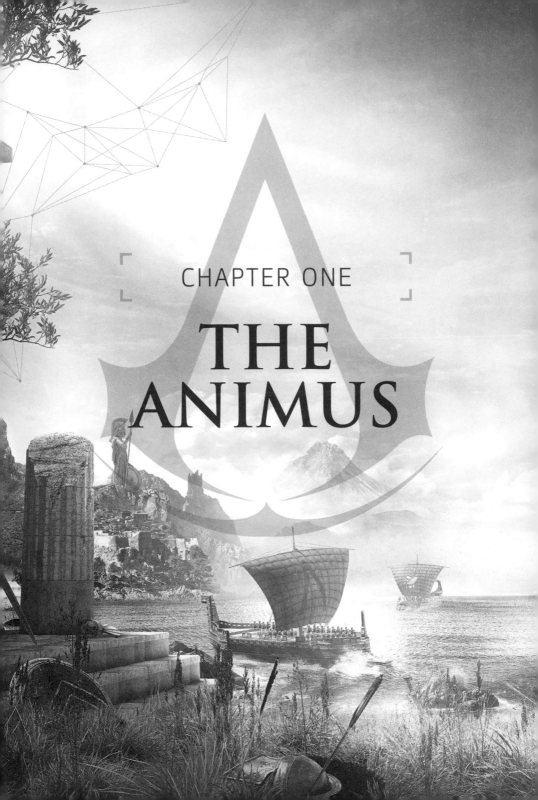

CHAPTER ONE

THE ANIMUS

The footsteps came closer and I closed my eyes, as if that would help me stay out of sight. They burst back open when a hand grabbed me from behind, covering my mouth. I tried to spin around, but the grip was too strong. Strong enough to drag me backward through what on the surface resembled a perfectly solid stone wall.

On the other side of the threshold, the assailant pushed a wooden structure covered in stone back into place with his spare hand. We were on the other side of a hidden entrance that led down some steep stairs. Fighting every urge to make noise, I finally managed to turn around as the hand was released from my face. It drew back toward a lightly bearded man with long, dark hair and covered his mouth with a single finger.

"Shhh."

I nodded as the man beckoned down the stairs. It seemed wise to do as my saviour said. There was a modicum of light; old-fashioned torches had been lit to show the way. I guessed that it must have been difficult to run electricity into a secret passage.

"We'll be safe in here for the moment, but I'd like to leave as soon as you've regained your composure," said the man.

"Who are you?"

"I'm Colm and I work for the good guys."

"That's what someone who works for the bad guys says," I retorted.

Colm paused and smirked. "How's 'I'm not currently trying to kill you, like those guys' work for you?"

"That works very well," I conceded. "I'm Joey."

Nodding with a remarkable calm that I certainly didn't feel, Colm must have decided that I was ready to continue. He led me through a long passage.

"Aren't you going to ask any questions?" he said, clearly inviting them.

"I'm more concerned about the noise until we're out of here," I replied, glancing nervously over my shoulder.

"Oh, we're fine in here," Colm confirmed. He shouted to prove it, while I involuntarily flinched.

"Fair enough. Who are you? Who are they? Why me? Did I see the future? What's that blade?"

"Do you still have it?"

"And there was me thinking you'd answer my questions, rather than ask one back."

"Sorry... but the blade. Do you have it?"

"Yes."

"Good. Keep it close. We're nearly out. Until we get to my car, we need to stay silent again."

"Sounds like a convenient way of not answering my questions," I noted.

Colm put his finger to his mouth again and opened a metal gate, which led out into a graveyard. The secret entrance was disguised as a crypt. Perhaps it even doubled as one. In hindsight, perhaps I should have exercised a little more caution at this stage but, instead, I blindly followed Colm to his car – and, hopefully, to some answers.

After a 20-minute drive – during which Colm continued to evade my questions – we pulled into an underground car park that led to an innocuous-looking basement. Inside were stacks and stacks of servers, all connected to what looked like a bed in the centre of the room.

"We call this the Animus. That vision you spoke about... seeing the future... this does something similar, only you'll have more control when you're in there."

I stared at him in a mix of wonder, confusion and disbelief until a woman entering

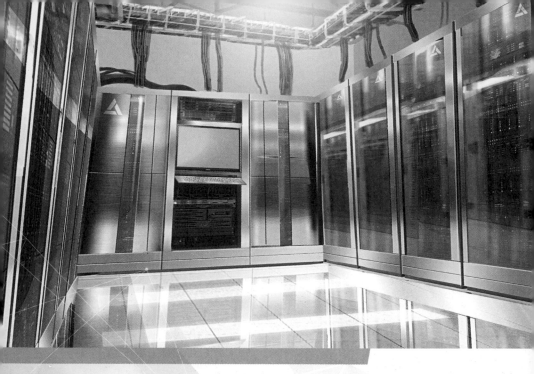

the basement distracted me. Instantly, I felt my fight or flight kick in and I sprung to the defensive.

"It's OK, this is my partner, Alera," Colm reassured me.

"Hi. Alera – that's an unusual name."

"Unless you have had it all your life," she responded, her accent placing her as perhaps European, or maybe even Far Eastern. "Do you have any reservations? Or are you ready for revelations?"

Her cryptic, poetic language somehow gave me confidence, even if I still had no idea about what was going on, so I followed her gesture to the Animus and sat on the edge.

She continued, "I advise you to lie down and close your eyes. You will experience the lives of certain people within the history of memories we have extracted from various individuals."

"Animus? Latin for 'the mind', isn't it?" I recalled.

"Among other things," she replied, seemingly impressed. "Spirit. Consciousness. Courage. Even anger. This device contains it all. Are you ready to see?"

I looked over at Colm for reassurance. I still didn't really know what I was getting myself in for. Alera was far more urgent and demanding than him, and I felt pressured to give an immediate answer. He nodded. What else could I do? I returned the nod.

"Good. Lie back," Alera insisted.

"So I'm going to experience lives? What do I do? Why do I have to do it?"

Colm stepped forward. "You'll know it when you see it. And as for the rest of the questions..."

He was interrupted as my vision erupted into a string of artificial shapes and code. It quickly faded to nothing, and the computer program that was running my experience gradually loaded in forms that became rocks

18

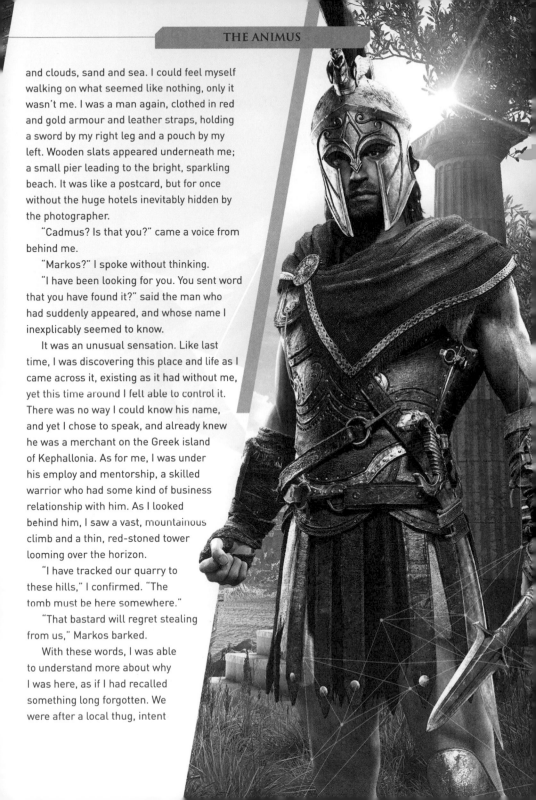

and clouds, sand and sea. I could feel myself walking on what seemed like nothing, only it wasn't me. I was a man again, clothed in red and gold armour and leather straps, holding a sword by my right leg and a pouch by my left. Wooden slats appeared underneath me; a small pier leading to the bright, sparkling beach. It was like a postcard, but for once without the huge hotels inevitably hidden by the photographer.

"Cadmus? Is that you?" came a voice from behind me.

"Markos?" I spoke without thinking.

"I have been looking for you. You sent word that you have found it?" said the man who had suddenly appeared, and whose name I inexplicably seemed to know.

It was an unusual sensation. Like last time, I was discovering this place and life as I came across it, existing as it had without me, yet this time around I felt able to control it. There was no way I could know his name, and yet I chose to speak, and already knew he was a merchant on the Greek island of Kephallonia. As for me, I was under his employ and mentorship, a skilled warrior who had some kind of business relationship with him. As I looked behind him, I saw a vast, mountainous climb and a thin, red-stoned tower looming over the horizon.

"I have tracked our quarry to these hills," I confirmed. "The tomb must be here somewhere."

"That bastard will regret stealing from us," Markos barked.

With these words, I was able to understand more about why I was here, as if I had recalled something long forgotten. We were after a local thug, intent on his "get rich quick" scheme of taking from others and selling the stolen goods to the highest bidder. We weren't yet sure of his identity, only that he had taken a parchment from us that indicated the location of a treasure, buried within a tomb, and he had followed its instructions to here.

"At least he has done some of the work," I acknowledged.

"So he has taken the map the last step of the way. It doesn't mean he is entitled to what is there."

"But I do not know where they are heading."

"You're good at climbing. Get up there and see if the view is better. If we don't deliver the item to our client, we will have more than our debt to them to worry about."

"Who is our client, Markos?"

"I told you, I don't know their name. I get our instructions through someone else to protect them. All I know is that their middleman is called Ianthe. Now get up there."

Markos pointed at the tower behind him. It was enormous and imposing, but my own fear of heights was overruled by Cadmus's clear experience and skill at ascending cliffs and structures like this. He skipped up the cliff-face like it was a walk in the park. How this was normal for him I couldn't quite tell, but it seemed natural to run up the sheer face and cling on to the smallest of protrusions. Reaching the top, I clambered over the edge and eyed up the smooth surface of the tower. This would be more difficult. I knew that any hold that had a crack on would not hold me. I sketched down a rough drawing of them on a parchment from my pouch, noting the letters engraved in the tower, and also estimating how far I believed I could make it for each jump. I could somehow tell that, knowing my own limitations and judging the holds that would take my weight, there was only one route up to the tower.

! SOLVE TO PASS

I began my ascent. When I made it to the top and had collected letters that made up a word, I knew I could proceed

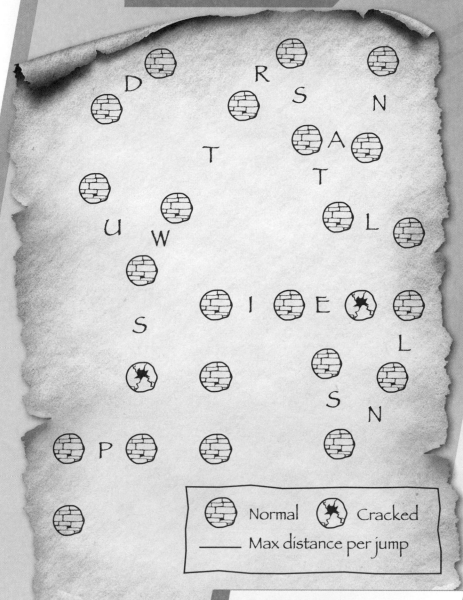

Normal — Cracked
Max distance per jump

FOR **DIFFICULT** HINTS, TURN TO PAGE **156**
FOR **MEDIUM** HINTS, TURN TO PAGE **166**
FOR **EASY** HINTS, TURN TO PAGE **176**
FOR **SOLUTIONS**, TURN TO PAGE **186**

I gripped the wall, advancing from hold to hold with my legs firmly in place, and to my surprise I seemed to sail up. It was exhilarating – the wind rushing past me, teasing me into thinking that it might whip my legs out from under me, while lifting me up the wall at the same time, as much a help as a hindrance. The physical excursion had me almost out of breath, but once I reached the top I knew I could continue if I had to.

Once at the summit I posed and surveyed the horizon. An inch either way and I might fall to my death, yet I felt empowered. The view was such that I could see clearly for miles. There was a village across the water where people were noisily going about their everyday tasks, as well as sparkling reflections from objects dotted around the landscape glinting back at me. Some activity, where people and animals were wandering, caught my eye. Ah, there they were. Up in the hills was a small troupe of armed mercenaries – six perhaps – moving slowly but steadily across a thin strip of rock toward what looked from below like a simple overcrop, but from here was clearly an entrance.

I had found it: the tomb. I looked down, expecting the vertigo that I had experienced on occasion in my real life, yet felt nothing but confidence. My body twinged in anticipation when I spotted a large pile of hay below. Surely not. Surely I – or Cadmus – couldn't be considering jumping?

I hesitated, and Cadmus did too. He shook his head, as if his own reluctance had taken him by surprise. I had control, but I also had his instincts and, at that moment, I had to trust he wouldn't be feeling OK with this without reason. I took the leap of faith.

The exercise and invigoration on the way up was nothing like the thrill of the way

down. I was calm, collected, almost serene. It was kind of like a rollercoaster I had ridden enough times to enjoy the sensation without raising my heart rate – this was fun!

I spun my legs over my head to land wide and spread my impact over as much of the hay as possible. It caught me effortlessly, barely scratching me as it brushed over my skin, and after a small bounce back up, I lay there, unhurt and satisfied with my aim. I jumped off and looked back at it. There was something funny about that hay...

Markos approached.

"They are up there," I confirmed, pointing to the location where I had seen the men.

"I'll... guard the area," said Markos nervously.

I smiled at his poor attempt to justify his cowardice. But if he could do it himself, why would he need my assistance?

Approaching the new rock-face, my climbing skills were put to use once again, though in smaller bursts this time as I moved from platform to platform. While I ascended once again, the thought crossed my mind

The boss has given me some money to buy a new outfit for him to wear today. He insists I use the entire amount as a test for me. I must buy a bracelet, some sandals, a tunic and a necklace for him. But what is the perfect combination I can afford?

1 Drachma (d) = 6 Oboli (o).

100 Drachma (d) = 1 Mine (m).

The stores at the market have promised me the following prices:

Leather Necklace	23d, 2o
Wool Necklace	13d, 2o
Leather Bracelet	30d, 5o
Wool Bracelet	20d, 5o
All types of Sandals	20d, 2o
Brown tunic	41d 4o
White tunic	43d 3o
Green tunic	45d
Blue tunic	46d 1o
Yellow tunic	50d

A

R

about the actual words I – or Cadmus – had spoken. Clearly at this time, in this place, Markos and the man whose memories I inhabited would not have been speaking my language. My experience of understanding his world must have extended to the very language I used. In some way I couldn't quite explain, I was comfortable here. Was the machine translating for me, or giving me actual understanding that extended beyond a mere simulation?

My train of thought ended when I reached the platform by the entrance. I saw that the people before me had lit torches to illuminate the tomb. I turned around and looked down but Markos wasn't visible from my position, so I headed towards the near-darkness of the entrance.

It seemed they had rolled a boulder out of the way to enter. No wonder they needed such a large group of mercenaries. By the entrance, there was a pile of discarded supplies on a crate next to a note. Considering this, I decided that it implied that the men were setting up for something more than just a quick look around.

I quietly and carefully entered, squeezing through the narrow passage and listening for any indication of those who had entered before me. All I could hear, though, was a sudden rumbling from where I had come from. They were sealing me in!

I ran backward as quickly as I could, just in time to see the last glimmer of light fade. It was a trap and I had fallen straight into it. I spun back around, with only one option: to press forward and hope that there was another way out. I grabbed one of the torches that was leaning against the wall and continued into a larger, multi-level chamber. There were more torches, ladders already in place and evidence of a campsite. They had been here for some time, yet they wanted to lock me in, rather than out. Why?

At the other end of the open area was a flat wall that looked like it had been carved with symbols and notches. I looked across and noted that there were holes below each symbol, which looked suspiciously like the torches scattered around might fit into them. All of the information I had seen previously had led me to this point, and my experiences of the recent past must have been for a purpose beyond dying in a cave.

 SOLVE TO PASS

I had three torches and, when I knew which of the slots to put them in, I knew I could proceed.

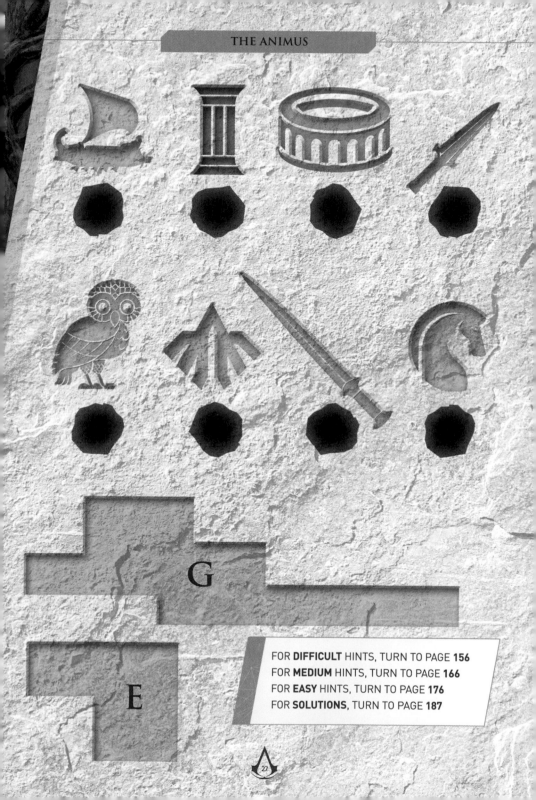

G

E

FOR **DIFFICULT** HINTS, TURN TO PAGE **156**
FOR **MEDIUM** HINTS, TURN TO PAGE **166**
FOR **EASY** HINTS, TURN TO PAGE **176**
FOR **SOLUTIONS**, TURN TO PAGE **187**

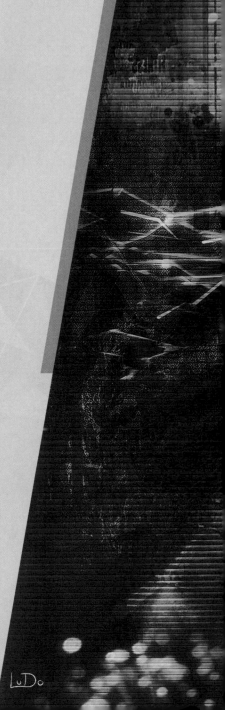

After placing the three torches correctly, an advanced mechanism began to rumble. The wall began to slide open, revealing a dark, stone entrance. I could feel fear well up in Cadmus, something that had not happened before. He was apparently fine with scaling an incredibly high wall, but something as mechanically simple from my time as a hidden door opening was well beyond his experience.

The walls were no longer natural and jagged but smooth, straight and angular. I stepped through the threshold and looked up at a wondrous sight. Inside the depths of the mountain, I entered what felt like a hidden world, not unlike my own experience of entering this one through the Animus. There was was a circular podium ahead of me. It sprang to life, illuminating itself in gold and blue. To me, it was impressive. To Cadmus, it must have been downright otherworldly. A holographic image of a woman appeared, floating in front of me, and spoke to Cadmus.

"Do not be afraid. I am here to help you."

"Who are you, and how are you doing this?" Cadmus asked desperately.

"Who I am is not important. I am of the race called Isu. We are the Precursors, Those Who Came Before, The First Civilization."

"I do not understand."

"This is not for you to understand," the woman announced piercingly. "You are not alone here."

"There is no one else in this place," Cadmus contradicted.

"You are incorrect. You have a spectator."

Cadmus span around, looking for anyone else around, but I wrestled to stop him. I knew the woman was talking about me.

"Ahead, you will find an item that you must keep safe. This is a piece of our civilization. A Piece of Eden. Your civilization must be kept

LuDo

safe for the good of us all. Only you can protect this place and allow us all to live on."

Cadmus stayed silent and, instead, I spoke out through him. "I saw a man called Malcolm."

"He is not just one of you humans. He is The Connection and his actions will lead to the destruction of all, should you let the Piece of Eden fall into his hands. Split it up and take the pieces far away."

I had spent the majority of time since I had woken up in the museum with endless questions but, now that I was faced with someone that may be able to answer them, I didn't know where to start. Unfortunately, my hesitation lasted too long and the woman disappeared.

"Who's there?" Cadmus shouted.

I didn't know if he was speaking to me or if he still assumed there was someone else in the cave with him. After a moment of silence, he stepped forward toward where the woman had indicated.

There was what looked like a container in his vision, with a keypad on top of it. There was no way all of this technology could have existed millennia ago. I looked around to see if I could find any indication of a code, then closer again at the keypad. It didn't have numbers or symbols on it. In fact, it just looked like blank buttons except for one, which contained an X. I reached out to touch it, and it illuminated.

Cadmus jumped back in shock; this experience was affecting him more than me, even though we were as one. I touched another button on the opposite side of the keypad and

the whole thing flashed red and made a painful, synthetic noise. Whatever I had done was clearly incorrect. I tried again. Touching buttons next to each other generally seemed fine, but not always. Looking closer, I noticed some seemed to have a thicker line separating them.

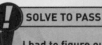

SOLVE TO PASS

I had to figure out the correct code. Once I had a path through all of the buttons, I knew I could proceed.

FOR **DIFFICULT** HINTS, TURN TO PAGE **156**
FOR **MEDIUM** HINTS, TURN TO PAGE **166**
FOR **EASY** HINTS, TURN TO PAGE **176**
FOR **SOLUTIONS**, TURN TO PAGE **187**

31

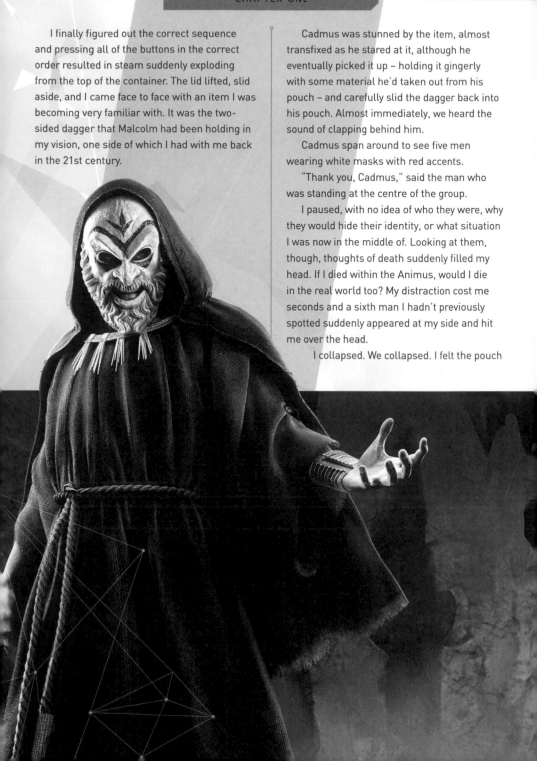

I finally figured out the correct sequence and pressing all of the buttons in the correct order resulted in steam suddenly exploding from the top of the container. The lid lifted, slid aside, and I came face to face with an item I was becoming very familiar with. It was the two-sided dagger that Malcolm had been holding in my vision, one side of which I had with me back in the 21st century.

Cadmus was stunned by the item, almost transfixed as he stared at it, although he eventually picked it up – holding it gingerly with some material he'd taken out from his pouch – and carefully slid the dagger back into his pouch. Almost immediately, we heard the sound of clapping behind him.

Cadmus span around to see five men wearing white masks with red accents.

"Thank you, Cadmus," said the man who was standing at the centre of the group.

I paused, with no idea of who they were, why they would hide their identity, or what situation I was now in the middle of. Looking at them, though, thoughts of death suddenly filled my head. If I died within the Animus, would I die in the real world too? My distraction cost me seconds and a sixth man I hadn't previously spotted suddenly appeared at my side and hit me over the head.

I collapsed. We collapsed. I felt the pouch

being wrestled from our side.

The pain I felt gave me a sudden, and very unwelcome, realization. It appeared that the more influence I had over Cadmus, the more his sensation felt like they were happening to me. Unfortunately, just at that moment, I had been exerting a considerable amount of influence. As I groaned with pain, the group turned around and strolled back through the doorway.

"Goodbye," said the leader, throwing a pot that looked to be filled with oil over his shoulder. It smashed and the liquid splashed around the entrance. Almost immediately, flames leaped from the torches marking the entry, swiftly enveloping our most direct means of escape.

I staggered to my feet, more shaken than hurt now, thinking frantically about finding another way out. The patterns of the flagstones in the floor indicated this was just one of three entrances to the central Isu structure. I swiftly headed in one of the other directions, but the flagstone path ended in a large hexagonal pattern and a smooth blank wall. I searched desperately, but could find no markings to help me, and try as I might I could not make sense of the hexagonal pattern. The heat was becoming intense, and I ran in the other direction, only to be confronted by another wall. But... this one had a hexagonal indent in it! It looked like it could be some kind of button or release mechanism

This was beyond Cadmus, but technology like this wasn't beyond me. I tried pushing against the indent and, despite nothing moving, it seemed to somehow sense my presence because it began to illuminate. Almost instantly, a rumbling came from the hexagonal floor. It started to rise up, like a giant elevator. I rushed toward it, leaping to catch the edge, and I managed to haul myself up onto the platform.

Looking above me, I was suddenly panicked by the thought that, if the hexagon didn't stop its ascent, it would crush me into the ceiling. Luck – or something I didn't quite understand – was on my side. The floor slowed down and came to a halt. I spotted an alcove nearby and Cadmus's training kicked in. I threw myself in the direction of the alcove and landed cleanly on the edge. Tracing the path around a corner led to more light. Natural light! I had found another route out.

I emerged into daylight by squeezing through of a small gap in a rock. My instincts were to climb up to get a lay of the land but I knew that my attackers were further down the hillside and I wanted to waste no time. Instead, I sprang from rock to rock, scrambling downhill until I was closer to where I thought they would be. Instead, Markos appeared.

"Cadmus? You are out! Did you find it?"

"I did, but I was ambushed by some men in strange masks."

"Ianthe will be so angry with us."

"The representative of our client?"

"Yes, indeed."

"Those men made a mistake by leaving me alive."

I squinted to better survey our environment, still re-adjusting to the brightness of the outside world, while feeling the anger rising inside of me. I blinked, and spotted some movement in the distance. It was my attackers heading toward the nearby town.

"I will follow them and make them pay," I announced and began the acrobatics that Cadmus was skilled in to propel me toward the group. Death-defying leaps and Olympic-level gymnastics allowed me to catch up with the men as they entered the town, attempting to

blend in with the crowd. The clank of weapons was overcome by the sound of horse hooves and of merchants noisily offering their wares.

I scrambled onto the rooftops for both a better view and a quicker path, and saw the coats the mercenaries had been wearing bundled up in a pile on the road, with their stack of masks pressing through the material from below. How would I now identify them?

I could see a suspicious-looking group up ahead, glancing nervously around as if they feared that they were being followed. From my

position above them, I could take one of them out and, if it was their leader, the rest might flee. But I didn't fancy my chances against all five of them.

Hang on, was I really considering killing for this blade? This whole situation seemed bigger than me, Cadmus, or even the Isu woman that had spoken to me. She had warned that I couldn't let them keep the blade or, perhaps, my vision of Malcolm would come true. And not just that. What had she said? "The destruction of all."

As I stared at them, I realized that everything I had experienced thus far in Kephallonia pointed toward one of the men I could see being the leader.

SOLVE TO PASS

I had to assassinate him, and only when I was sure I had the right one did I know I could proceed.

FOR **DIFFICULT** HINTS, TURN TO PAGE **156**
FOR **MEDIUM** HINTS, TURN TO PAGE **166**
FOR **EASY** HINTS, TURN TO PAGE **176**
FOR **SOLUTIONS**, TURN TO PAGE **187**

I recognized the blue shirt and, almost the second I did, the man looked up at me and started running. This was all the confirmation I needed. I clambered over the rooftops, crossing streets by balancing fearlessly on ropes strung between the buildings, trying to head him off before he was able to escape. He ducked through alleyways but following the weaving paths of the streets at ground level, he was slower than the direct path I was using.

He entered a small courtyard with a fountain in the centre and launched over the front lip, desperate to move as fast as possible, but I was already there, hopping down on a series of posts that led right up to the statue atop the fountain. As he ran below me, I matched his speed and jumped so as to land directly on top of him. He must have heard me, or sensed me above him, because he looked up as I fell toward him and pulled the dagger up to meet me. One blade was pointed toward him and one blade toward me. The inevitability of gravity meant that, although I tensed up and tried to readjust my trajectory while in mid-air, I was falling right towards him.

Time seemed to slow down but I felt no panic. I shifted my body as much as I could until, suddenly, I slammed down onto his arm. The blade slid beside me, scratching my flesh painfully but not fatally, while the other half pierced his skin in an almost gentle fashion for something so deadly. He looked up at me and I back at him, as the rest of the world grew silent around us.

Breaking away from our mutual stare, I noticed that the simulation had changed. I was in a blank void with the man.

"I am but a small part of the machine," he spat at me, leering vilely.

He was in no pain, had no injury. But he was dying, we both knew it, and I hoped that the inevitability of his death would give him an honesty that I would not otherwise expect from my adversary.

"Who are you?" Cadmus asked. I had a horrible feeling that I already knew.

"Ianthe. I am your client."

"What? I thought you were merely a representative... If you hired us, why would you to go the trouble of stealing the map? And why try to kill me... lock me in that place?"

"This item is more than just a trinket. It is more than just value. The mere knowledge of its existence is something we cannot allow. That's why you had to die."

"So you used us to find it, knowing you would never fulfil your side of the agreement."

"We have a greater cause, you and I, and sometimes we do not know the machine we are a part of."

Ianthe faded into dust in front of my eyes. I did not know what had just happened. Perhaps the simulation, in the moment of his passing, gave me access to his innermost thoughts, just for a moment? Whatever had happened, I was back in the courtyard, double-sided dagger in hand, wondering what it could all mean. The rush of a blade coming toward me broke my focus and I rolled out of the way. The other four men had seen Ianthe's death, and their reactions were varied. Two ran instantly but two remained. A spritely, wispy-bearded fellow and a large, round-headed man surrounded me.

The huge one lunged at me, weaponless, and, without breaking a sweat, I stepped aside and caught his leg, sending him to the ground. Before I could react further, the smaller man's blade came at me again. I whirled around, defending with the dagger. With a huge clang, it split into two, one side still in my hands and the other flying across the courtyard toward the giant. He turned, just in time to catch it with his face, the blade embedded deeply within his left eye. He screamed out in pain and collapsed back to the floor.

The smaller man looked around, wondering what to do. His decision was, I thought, to help the other man as I slowly backed away. I had forgotten the importance of the blade. He tore the blade from his companion's eye and ran, leaving his friend half-blinded forevermore.

He was quick.

By the time I realized that I should be chasing him, Cadmus had already begun

running for me. Unfortunately, the other man's athletics rivalled mine, step for step. He darted through windows, as if he knew every step of where he was running to: a dock with a ship already in motion. He leaped from the dock onto the moving ship and it turned away from the shore toward the vibrant horizon. Desperately, I jumped toward the vessel but I fell short with a splash. My swimming could not match the power of the ship's sails and it easily evaded my reach.

The man called out as he sailed away. "You cannot stop the inevitable. This is for the good of all. In the end, you will learn that, by following us, everybody benefits."

The ship's sails were white, with red accents, matching the colours of the masks I had seen earlier, and the image burned into my head as I turned to swim back to shore. Markos was standing on the dock, looking at the ship as it grew smaller. He help me up from the water.

"Who was that? What was he saying?" Markos asked.

"That was one of our clients, claiming that, if we worked together, everybody would benefit."

"You know, perhaps he's right?"

"You can't think that, after betraying us, we should work with them again?"

"No. But look. We were in debt to them and now they run from us."

"Us?"

"Well, you."

"Now, surely, they won't come back, which means our debt has gone and they have what

they want. And by the look of things, we gained something else too." Markos gestured down to the single blade I had retained. "See? Everybody benefits."

I wasn't quite sure that Markos had the right idea, but it had sparked a sense of optimism in him that I hadn't seen beforehand. Or perhaps it was just opportunism?

"We could sell that and finally have some money to spend," he continued.

"We're not selling this. I believe it is too valuable and, by the sound of things, it should be kept from those masked men at all cost."

"Shame. The things I could do with the money. You know I have always wanted to establish a vineyard."

"That can wait, Markos." I smiled. "I think I should leave this place."

"What? But we're finally making some profit. What am I going to do without you? I need an apprentice."

"Apprentice? Is that what I am?"

Markos shrugged his shoulders, playfully.

"I'm sure you'll find another apprentice, my friend," I joked.

Both of us smiled and looked out over the vista in front of us. After a few moments, we turned and headed back toward town. An electronic shimmering sound filled my ears and, when I looked to see where it was coming from, I saw the mountains and sea in the distance gradually disintegrating into pixels. I was being pulled out of the simulation.

I was leaving the Animus.

CHAPTER TWO

TRAINING

"Are you OK?" Colm gently murmured.

"That was intense," I replied. "Completely vivid."

"I wish we could take credit for the technology," came the voice of Alera from near a control panel. "We had to pull you out. Some of our stuff can be a little temperamental."

Almost on cue, a shower of sparks erupted above her. She barely flinched, clearly used to the occasional exploding of electronics by now.

"I'll get another fuse," she announced, strolling out of the room.

"That's quite some simulation."

Colm paused, leaned over to a nearby table and picked up an apple as I spun my legs around to sit up straight. He tossed the apple to me, but I fumbled it and it fell to the floor. I bent over to pick it up, brushed it off and then took a bite.

"Joey, what you experienced just then, it's more than just a simulation. They're your memories now. You really lived them," Colm insisted.

"But what if I did something that didn't really happen?" I spluttered through chunks of half-chewed fruit.

"Then you get desynchronized."

"What? Is that dangerous?" It sounded dangerous.

"Not really. It's rare, but sometimes your mind will take you off in the wrong direction; fail at something you didn't fail at or miss an important piece of information that the person definitely did not miss. In this case, the simulation of the memory will destabilize and eject you from it."

"Is that what just happened?"

"No. That was us bringing you out. You'd found what we needed and there was no sense in wasting more of your time."

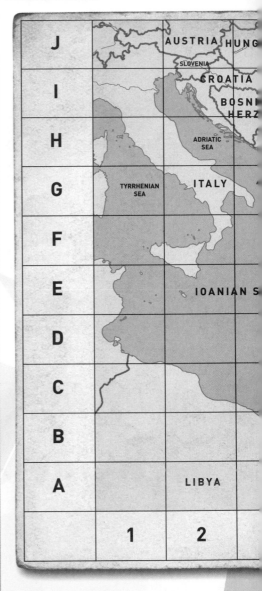

"Wasting? It was incredible. I'd choose to spend time there."

Colm raised his eyebrows. "Indeed. There is a commercialization of the technology that already exists. You must have heard of

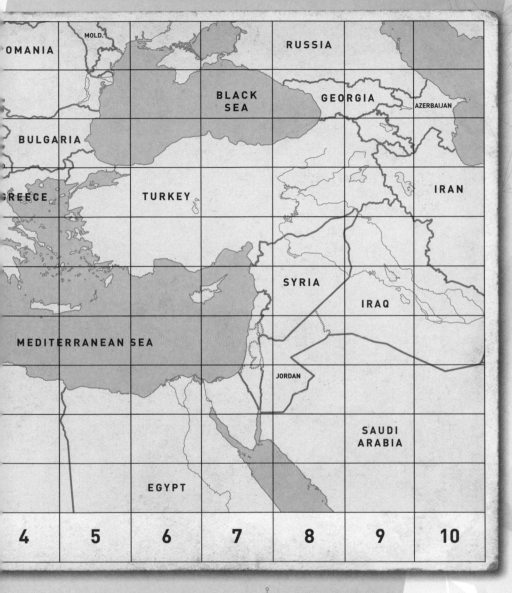

ROMANIA

MOLD.

RUSSIA

BLACK
SEA

GEORGIA

AZERBAIJAN

BULGARIA

GREECE

TURKEY

IRAN

SYRIA

IRAQ

MEDITERRANEAN SEA

JORDAN

SAUDI
ARABIA

EGYPT

| 4 | 5 | 6 | 7 | 8 | 9 | 10 |

Abstergo Entertainment." It was more of a question than a statement.

"The games company?" I sighed as the pictures starting to fall into place. "So, what did I find that you needed?"

"The man who took the other half of the blade. We can use the information you witnessed to track him out of Greece and find out where the blade ended up," Colm proudly stated, pointing at a section of a world map on the wall.

"So, you mentioned synchronization. Surely any little thing I chose to do that's different from Cadmus would ruin that."

"It's more like a motorway. Even if you change lanes, you're still heading in the right direction. The memory can be mis-remembered and it will still end up in the right place, as long as you don't do something drastic, like turn the vehicle around and drive into oncoming traffic. But it's remarkably hard to get off course."

"Why? What if I'd not gone in the cave? Or asked Markos to do it?"

"You wouldn't. Life is remarkably deterministic."

"But now I might. Now I might try to test that theory."

"Think of it like choosing what to eat for lunch," Colm explained. "Say you have the option of a piece of cake or an apple. You may have had a hard day or achieved something great and treat yourself to the cake, or maybe you've just been to the doctor and are thinking of being a little healthier. These decisions come from

our past. Now, say you're thinking about this conversation, so you decide to change your decision to break from determinism. You've done that because of this conversation. Another event in your past."

"You think free will doesn't exist?"

"I'm not saying that. I'm just saying that the decisions you make because of your free will are determined by your experiences and history. Your past. These memories are the same. You gain the experiences and life of Cadmus, or whomever we find next, and you're likely to behave how they did."

I sat in silence, thinking both about

what it all meant and of how deep this conversation had become.

"Anyway," Colm cut through the silence, tearing a piece of paper from a nearby machine, "here's the information we learned from your memory about the man that left with the blade."

4 G ꟼ
8 I D
8 E +
6 A ꟻ
4 D ꓭ

FOR **DIFFICULT** HINTS, TURN TO PAGE **157**
FOR **MEDIUM** HINTS, TURN TO PAGE **167**
FOR **EASY** HINTS, TURN TO PAGE **177**
FOR **SOLUTIONS**, TURN TO PAGE **188**

I stared blankly at the printout, half-expecting Colm to offer me an explanation.

"Numbers and symbols?" I asked.

"Do you recognize the symbols?"

"We believe they are from an ancient language," called Alera as she re-entered the room, brandishing what was probably the largest fuse I had ever seen.

"I think I've seen it before," I said.

"That's not possible," she replied.

"No, really," I insisted. "I could swear that I saw a wall of letters like that as a child."

Alera turned away, trying to shut down the conversation. Colm looked interested – intrigued – but spotted Alera's reaction and seemed to think better of it.

Alera ripped out the old fuse and slammed the new one in place, with a lack of delicacy that concerned me. The lights went out, plunging us into pitch blackness for a few

seconds, until the whirring of a generator kicked in and brought the main lights back up.

"All good now. Ready to go back in?" she said forcefully.

"We don't know where we're going yet," Colm replied.

"What were you talking about while I was out of the room?"

I stayed silent. Something about Alera's demeanour concerned me.

"Glad to see we're all communicating," Alera continued sarcastically. "So you've seen these symbols before then? Why not draw what you remember on that chalkboard over there?"

Like a disruptive pupil being called to the front of the class I sheepishly stepped forward, picked up some chalk from under the board and let my hand draw what I remembered.

"What is that?" Colm asked.

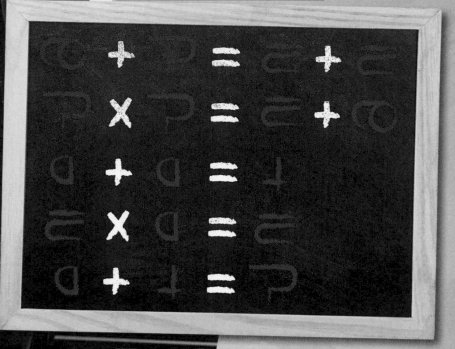

I shrugged, genuinely unsure until I thought about it further. "I think each left side equals the right side. Each symbol represents a number."

"Full of surprises then," Alera quipped.

Looking back over the information I had, I determined the next locations I would be heading to.

! SOLVE TO PASS

Once I knew the country, I knew I could proceed.

FOR **DIFFICULT** HINTS, TURN TO PAGE **157**
FOR **MEDIUM** HINTS, TURN TO PAGE **167**
FOR **EASY** HINTS, TURN TO PAGE **177**
FOR **SOLUTIONS**, TURN TO PAGE **188**

"Egypt. The man went to Egypt," I announced." Can we follow him? Is that possible?"

Colm beamed at me. "Oh, we can get you there, if you're ready?"

Perhaps my success had led to my enthusiasm. I nodded excitedly. I had never been to Egypt.

"How's 53 BCE?" Alera asked.

I laid back down on the Animus and closed my eyes, ready to dive into the past.

Sweltering heat greeted me. The kind of sun that looks great in staged photos when booking a vacation, but makes you regret your clothing choices. I realized I was considering my voyages like holidays, but I might as well enjoy them. I turned around to see a series of white buildings in the shadow of a pyramid that was around 25 meters high. The steps that made the walls were small but, despite only having the ridiculously sized iconic pyramids of Giza I'd seen on postcards to compare it to, it was still impressive.

"Have you never seen the Pyramid of Elephantine before?" came a voice from beside me. I'd not noticed the man until then due to my fascination with the view.

"I've never been this far south of the white walls of Memphis," I admitted, gradually filling out my own lack of knowledge of Egyptian geography with that of my host.

"You know why you are here, Khepri, and if you complete your training here, I will be able to take you to see him."

The man talking to me was – I somehow knew without knowing him – called Nashwa. He was adorned in a long, hooded coat, which managed to both stand out and blend him into a crowd. Khepri must be me, I thought: an athletic woman with a strong sense of justice and respect for tradition.

"Where is the island?" I questioned.

"Just south of here but, before we go there, we have one final trial."

"I thought the island was my final trial."

"This business is more important than a trial," Nashwa insisted. "Now ascend to the top of the pyramid to assess the area and see if you can find the cartographer."

"There are a lot of footholds that look like they'll give way."

"Is this a problem for you? I have seen your skills."

I shook my head. My training was clearly more advanced than Cadmus's. I felt lighter on

my feet and more agile I seemed to rocket up the pyramid.

I reached the top and surveyed the area. In the distance was the island I needed to head to: the Island of Philae. It was an impressive structure for such an isolated location. I looked to my left and saw the nearby town, Aswan.

Recalling information that Khepri had was a strange feeling, like cheating off someone in a test. I hadn't earned the knowledge but had become an expert on the time simply because of this simulation. Recalling that it was a simulation broke my concentration for a moment, and I felt Khepri shake her head to regain it. She looked back down at the houses and the whole environment seemed to glitch for a second, throwing symbols that I assumed were hieroglyphics into my vision.

A man in the streets stuck out to me. He was the cartographer that I needed to convince to provide a map of the area. He seemed to trip over a small animal – I assumed a chicken, but it was just a guess from my distance away. As he tripped, he lost his grip on a book full of individual papyrus pages. They were whipped up into the air by the strong wind, then circled and tumbled around the buildings. I waited for the pages to sway gently to the ground, but they rose higher and continued their dance in mid-air, floating above the buildings. My vision glitched again and some of the pages seemed to duplicate.

I instinctively knew that any duplicate pages couldn't be real. If I could avoid them, perhaps I could find a route to collect the rest for the cartographer.

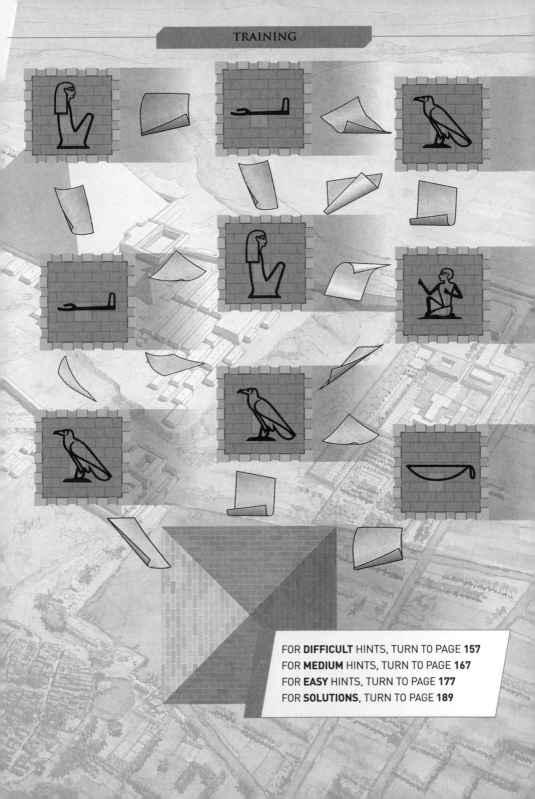

FOR **DIFFICULT** HINTS, TURN TO PAGE **157**
FOR **MEDIUM** HINTS, TURN TO PAGE **167**
FOR **EASY** HINTS, TURN TO PAGE **177**
FOR **SOLUTIONS**, TURN TO PAGE **189**

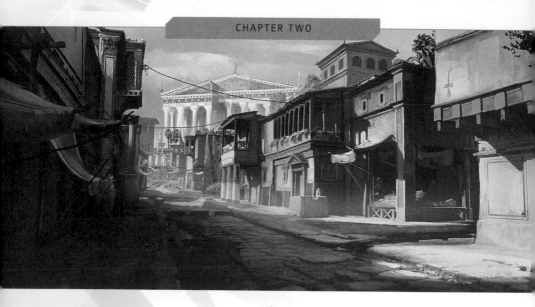

I swooped over, gathered up the pages and landed next to the man... and the chicken.

"That was quite impressive," he lauded. "I expect you're with Nashwa."

"And if I am?" I replied, passing the pages to him.

"Then you have earned what he has been asking for some time," he said smugly, handing over an open piece of parchment and turning away.

"Who are you?" I asked.

"My name? I deal in maps, my dear," calling out one final thing as he departed. "A name is but a series of labels for the back. What matters are the details on the front."

I looked at the parchment: a map of the Temple of Philae. This showed me the layout of where I was to visit. Nashwa suddenly landed next to me, with impressive stealth, and clasped his hands together in admiration.

"Your resourcefulness has paid off. Are you ready to visit the temple?"

"I am."

"Your target is The Medicine, a doctor from Memphis using the position of a healer to gather allies and despatch enemies. He is a bad man, and those protecting him do not deserve to live."

I nodded. "I understand."

"Your initiation to The Hidden Ones is complete. You have earned this," Nashwa announced.

He leaned over and fixed a small harness to my wrist. The device was connected to my upper arm by a hidden mechanism and when I extended my wrist a small, glistening blade was revealed. My heart skipped a beat as I looked down, excited to see something I was so familiar with, but as I looked closer, I realized it was not the same as the one from my vision or that I had found in the museum.

"This hidden blade will

allow you to despatch your enemies silently and efficiently," Nashwa began. "To get to The Medicine, you will need to assassinate all of their followers. If you are detected, things could get messy, and swimming back from the island will put you in a dangerous position. The crocodiles can smell blood from miles away. Do not get into conflict. Stealth is everything."

"I understand."

"This blade will no doubt assist you in your task. Are you sure you're up to it?"

"Do you think this is the first time I've killed people that deserved it?" I replied confidently.

Nashwa smiled and extended his arm toward the water in the direction of the island of Philae. I didn't hesitate before plunging into the water.

I swam quickly and smartly, avoiding the obvious crocodiles in the water, and noticed that one of them had strange markings on its back.

FOR **DIFFICULT** HINTS, TURN TO PAGE **157**
FOR **MEDIUM** HINTS, TURN TO PAGE **167**
FOR **EASY** HINTS, TURN TO PAGE **177**
FOR **SOLUTIONS**, TURN TO PAGE **189**

	1	2	3	4	5	6	7	8
〰〰〰	÷1	÷2	÷3	÷4	÷1	÷2	÷3	÷4
𓁹	–3	+8	–1	+4	–7	+5	–6	+2
⊓	+1	+2	+3	+4	+5	+6	+7	+8
🪲	+3	+3	+3	+3	+3	+3	+3	+3
𓂀	x3	x4	x1	x4	x2	x1	x3	x4
𓈖	+9	+4	+8	+2	+3	+1	+7	+5
🐦	–9	–8	–7	–6	–5	–4	–3	–2

I pulled myself up out of the water and waited a moment for the drips to subside. I would take any advantage I could to avoid leaving a suspicious trail or making noise. The temple was made of thick, uneven blocks – ideal for climbing up. I ascended as high as I could and walked over to an opening. On the other side was a beam, useful for me to walk over and assess the environment without being noticed.

I saw a host of guards around one locked door, where I imagined The Medicine would be hiding. Each guard was stationary and looking in a certain direction. I sketched their positions on the map, and where I assumed I could go without being seen. There must be an order, I thought, in which I could take out the guards without alerting any others to my presence, leaving just the final room unguarded. The room in question had a grid of letters and symbols on the door. On the walls inside the room were numbers, but I did not immediately know what they referred to.

I walked back over my route through the temple, above floor level, and realized that the symbols were also on small monoliths that each of the guards stood next to.

FOR **DIFFICULT** HINTS, TURN TO PAGE **158**
FOR **MEDIUM** HINTS, TURN TO PAGE **168**
FOR **EASY** HINTS, TURN TO PAGE **178**
FOR **SOLUTIONS**, TURN TO PAGE **189**

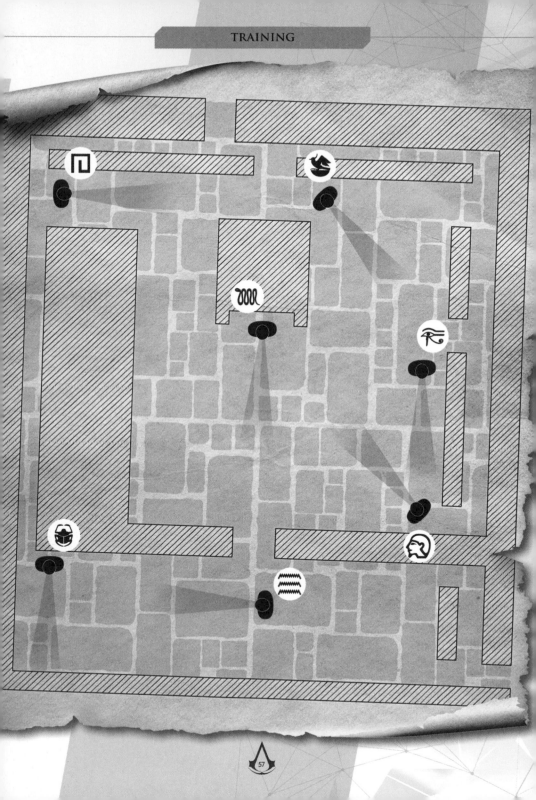

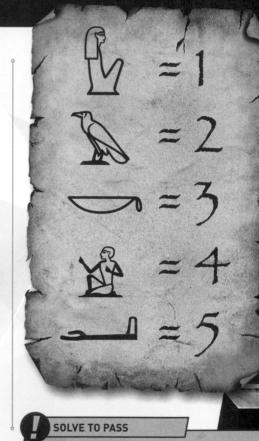

My instincts kicked in and observing everyone effectively allowed me to kill the guards without arousing suspicion. I was finally left with a door to my target. I tried the lock but it didn't budge, clearly secured from the inside. I felt a pang of frustration. Had I come this far only to be stopped by the simplest of defences?

No locks were present. The door had to have been barricaded and, without knowing the resources behind the door, I had no idea how long The Medicine could stay holed up. I had one main advantage, though, it was stealth. The Medicine had no idea that his guards were dead and, if I could convince him that I was one of them, he might open the door to me. If I had his name, I could call it out and, perhaps, that would be enough.

I paused for a second, wondering how I might be able to find it. The words of the cartographer hit me. Had I been so stupid as to overlook a simple clue? "A name is but a series of labels for the back." I turned the map over to find a list of hieroglyphs and seemingly random numbers. While I didn't have a clue what they meant, Khepri knew that this wasn't a translation. The hieroglyphs weren't related to the numbers at all but would give me the starting point to be able to call The Medicine's name.

! SOLVE TO PASS

Once I had discovered their true name, I knew I could proceed.

TRAINING

FOR **DIFFICULT** HINTS, TURN TO PAGE **158**
FOR **MEDIUM** HINTS, TURN TO PAGE **168**
FOR **EASY** HINTS, TURN TO PAGE **178**
FOR **SOLUTIONS**, TURN TO PAGE **189**

The name of The Medicine was Habibah? A woman? I realized that her guards were all men, so I put on my deepest voice and knocked, calling out her name. Seconds felt like minutes as I waited for a response, then, suddenly, a loud metallic clunk echoed around the temple. The door had been opened. I pushed through and came face to face with The Medicine, who was dressed in gold-and-white robes like some kind of pharaoh.

"Clever, very clever," she complimented. "I wasn't expecting a woman."

"Nor was I," I admitted.

"Do you think you can stop us all?"

"Right now, I only care that I can stop you." I lunged forward and pulled back my wrist,

exposing the glinting metal to her chest. I aimed perfectly for her heart and, before she could take a breath, I saw the light in her eyes go out. Time slowed – not just for her, but for me as well – and the simulation gave us a moment alone in the mist, just the two of us.

"I am genuinely impressed," she began. "It should not have ended like this."

"This is not over. Just over for you."

She laughed, a booming cackle, unexpected for a woman of her stature.

"Not just me. Do you know how many of you have tried to kill me?"

"I am not the first?"

"Was it Nashwa who sent you? These trials. I knew my end was inevitable. You can never

that they were idols here?"

"Cause and effect. They may not know they are idols here but, when people began congregating on an island – easy pickings for the hungry beast – it could have drawn them. Seeing the effect does not mean you necessarily understand the cause."

"You don't know why you're doing what you're doing?"

"That is faith, hidden one. Something I assume you have plenty of."

She smiled and blew away like ash. I was disarmed by her apparent contentment with her own demise, leaving me with questions that I may never have answers to. Her smugness would never be wiped from her smile now that she had ended the conversation.

I was back at the site of her death and looked over at the golden chest she had referred to. It was unlocked, so I pried it open to see a very recognizable item. The blade that we had been searching for, taken to Egypt from Greece so long ago by the man with the wispy beard. I held it in my hands and the power seemed to ripple through me.

win them all. It just takes one to catch you off guard. Look in my golden chest. You will see the trinkets I have kept from the rest."

"Do you think that matters to me?" I said, "I have done what must be done."

"It matters."

"Why do you all follow the cause you do?"

Habibah paused for a moment and seemed to revel in shocking me by blurting out her answer.

"Think of this temple. It was built and dedicated to Sobek, the crocodile god. Whether you believe in his powers or not, it is surrounded by them. But was the temple built here because of the crocodiles, or did the crocodiles come because of the temple?"

"You expect me to believe that they could tell

I did not know what it did, and neither did Khepri, but its significance was lost on neither of us. Before I could think any further, I heard movement in the corridor and was back on the defensive. Cruel eyes poked around the bottom of the doorway; a crocodile that had followed the scent of death to where I was. It saw me but lunged toward the easy prey: Habibah's body.

Despite my comfort with my own acts, something about an animal consuming human flesh was horrific and I waited for my moment to leap past it and climb back up to relative safety. The island was inhabited by more crocodiles now, each greedily enjoying the fruits of my work. I waited for my moment and splashed through the Nile back to the mainland.

Nashwa was waiting for me and nodded to me on my arrival, having watched the crocodile's migration with an understanding of what had taken place.

"You have proven yourself," he confirmed.

"I am not the first that tried to kill The Medicine, am I?"

"No. Does this bother you?"

"Only because I found this," I exclaimed, presenting the blade to Nashwa.

"It is a good job you have passed the trial."

"Why is that?" I posed.

"Because he will want to see both you and this blade now."

Nashwa and I headed to Memphis and to the man that I had heard so much about; the man who had led the Hidden Ones – the assassins – to where they were.

"My name is Bayek," he said by way of an introduction, "and you have done a lot of good."

"Thank you," I said humbly, quietened by my – or Khepri's – nerves.

"I have another task for you if you will do it?"

"Name it."

"So eager to follow. Do you fear the weight of your heart?"

"When you find a way to do some good, should you not put your all behind it?" I asked rhetorically.

Bayek smiled and turned to a large map behind him. "Devotion can so easily be misplaced. Where does yours lie?"

I thought for a second. Was he asking if I would follow him, or something deeper?

"To The Hidden Ones. To our order."

"Excellent. I believe you can do the most good by heading to Baghdad, setting up a home for The Hidden Ones there."

"Then it will be done."

Without a second's pause, Khepri turned and headed out the way she had come in. This was her, not me. She had a purpose and a drive beyond my own, and it was a pleasure to glimpse it. I knew that Nashwa and Bayek were proud of us, and while basking in the satisfaction of purpose, the simulation faded away.

"The weight of your heart?" asked Colm as I came to.

"You saw that?" I spluttered.

"You kept muttering the phrase."

Alera butted in, showing her knowledge in a way that came across more arrogantly than she had, I suspect, intended. "Ancient Egyptians believed that, upon death, it was the weight of their heart that mattered the most."

"The weight of it?"

"Not literally," she continued. "They felt that the heart contained all of the good and bad that they had done. A person's true character. Your heart would be weighed against the feather of a goddess – Maat."

"Isn't Matt a male name?" Colm joked.

"Maat. There are two As. If your heart weighed more than the feather, a monster would eat it. No paradise for you."

I had had enough of the side-track.

"So, the second blade went to Baghdad," I blurted out.

"Good work," Colm reassured. "I guess it's time to pick up the trail."

FOLLOWING THE TRAIL

Time off. It didn't seem appropriate to relax when the stakes seemed so high. But were they really? My vision of the future wasn't due to come true any time soon, but apparently the men trying to kill me at the museum could be "hot on our tails", whatever that meant. I tried to reason that they had no time to delay and, if they knew where we were, there was nothing to stop them finding us right away. Alera's words echoed around my head while lounging in my hotel room.

"They *will* find us. It is an inevitability, not a possibility."

When, not if. We simply had to locate the current whereabouts of the blade by then. Colm was busy exploring any records of Baghdad from a time that I couldn't work out a better name for than "the zero-th century". I, however, was ordered to rest. Apparently, my work in the Animus could have undesirable effects, but I was feeling fine. Invigorated actually. The only trouble was that, no matter how much my bed felt like I was being eaten by a cloud, that couldn't override the excitement of what I was a part of, and what exotic location and time I would visit next. Insomnia was a devastating paradox; becoming more tired while being unable to sleep. I was pleased to hear my phone ring.

"Hello?" I answered.

"Joey. It's Colm. I hope you're well rested."

"Not really."

"It doesn't particularly matter," he admitted.

"Then why the need for the break?"

"It's the break that's important. Not the rest. Also, I needed to find a lead. Head on back," he ordered.

I complied, walking back into the Animus chamber with as much wonder as the first time.

Alera jumped to attention, calling out to me, "Your work in the first century was good, but you'll need to be better this time."

Of course. That's what it was called.

"You're nodding," she continued. "Then you're ready. Take a look at this."

She threw a metal cylinder at me. I shifted my weight almost instantly and stepped to the side, holding my hand where my head was and catching the object in a strong grasp that seemed to impress even Alera.

"I guess something's rubbing off," I boasted.

Colm and Alera shared an alarmed look. Perhaps they realized that the balance of power was shifting slightly. If the men attacked again, I wondered if I would be the one to get the others out of any mess, as experiencing the lives of the two well-trained athletes had clearly allowed me to gain some of their skills.

"Just look at the tube," Colm deflected.

I unravelled it to find a parchment that seemed older than I felt I should be touching by hand.

"Don't worry," Alera started, "it's a reproduction. A translation really. A Templar artefact."

"Templar?" I wondered.

"Our enemies," Colm explained. "They've been around for as long as records began in one form or another. The men in masks that you saw in Greece were ancestors of The Order. Now they have a lot more reputable names. Abstergo, Wexell, all of the big corporations really. Not everybody that works for them knows what they're doing, but everyone in control is trying to... well... control."

The whole situation was a little beyond me but I nodded and looked down at the scroll. It was a series of sentences and instructions that did not immediately make sense to me. I flipped the parchment to see a map of the Far East.

"The Templars knew that this was important to the blade's location, even back then. But they did not know the starting point or the fact that

the contents held a hidden message. Somehow the secrets within stayed hidden and, before we put you back in, we need to figure out where to send you. This holds the key."

I looked down at the instructions again, wondering if it could explain where I was heading.

I started my journey at Yerevan, and visited Baghdad, then Burayday and ended at Dammam. My associate told me to make the tour of Ankara, Sharm El-Sheihk, Hail and Erzurum. I tried it, but was not keen on the route, so I visited them in a different order. Starting at Sharm El-Sheihk I wanted to finish at Erzurum, and visit Hail after Ankara.

Most of the year I spent in a round trip between Yerevan, Isfahan and Burayday.

When I had to change again, I took the tour

advised of my associate again.

I was tired by this point in the year, so I finished with Baghdad to Dammam, Burayday to Baghdad, and Dammam to Isfahan.

 SOLVE TO PASS

Once I knew the location of where I was going, I knew I could proceed

FOR **DIFFICULT** HINTS, TURN TO PAGE **159**
FOR **MEDIUM** HINTS, TURN TO PAGE **169**
FOR **EASY** HINTS, TURN TO PAGE **179**
FOR **SOLUTIONS**, TURN TO PAGE **190**

"London? But that's not even on the map."

"Of course," Colm gleefully offered. "That's why they never found it. They assumed it was on this map, but The Hidden Ones took it all the way to England."

"We only have one available source from even close to back then in London," Alera said worriedly.

"Ninth-century England," I mused. "The Vikings? Well, I was hoping for somewhere a little more tropical, but at least I already know the language," I joked.

I hopped over the railing by the table we were gathered around and slid into position on the Animus. I assumed the look that Alera and Colm shared was a jealous sigh, but it was much later when I realized that it was worry for what was happening to me. My newly found skills were the sign of a much deeper problem that I would face, but I was ignorant to it then and smiling as I closed my eyes to discover the excitement within the Animus in 873 CE.

I kicked a large chest, as my men helped to heave it open the strength of our combined force breaking the metal locks to reveal the spoils within. Gold, wood and other materials that would help us improve our homestead and secure our lives in this unforgiving and unfriendly country.

I called out to one of my men. "Einar, take these to our longboat. This will be enough for now."

"Of course," he replied. "Ingeborg was here earlier and said she had made this for you to help with the abbey."

I looked down at the small braid, made with a colourful pattern. It had to signify something but it was unclear to me yet.

Einar continued, "I shall return to the longboat, Alva."

I was Alva, adorned with braided hair and runic tattoos, the strength of my longboat crew allowing us to conquer where many had failed before us. I left the small and filthy hut to see a rich green landscape peppered with buildings and an impressive belltower attached to an immodest abbey. My instinct returned to ascend it and, as quick as a flash, I came to its base and assessed my route up.

I knew my skills were improving now. If I leaped powerfully and quickly, I could probably pass over one of the cracked footholds without it collapsing under me, but the power required for it would exhaust me. Perhaps doing this once in my ascent was the best I could do.

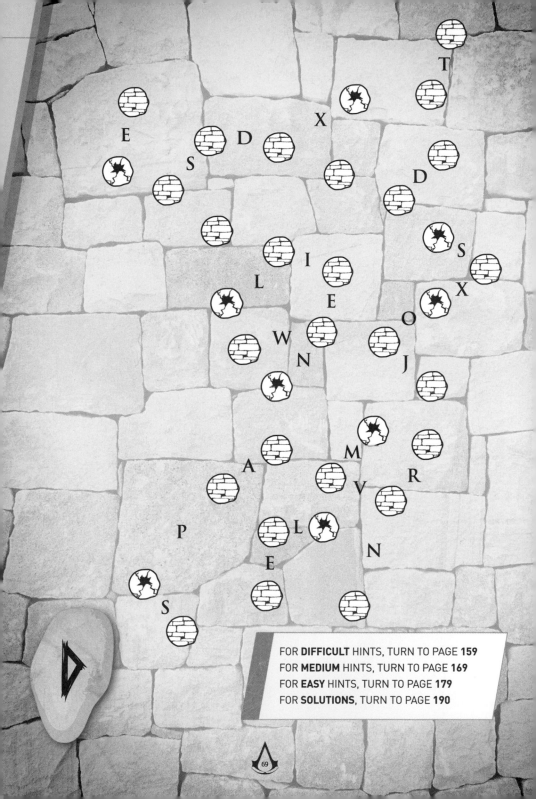

FOR **DIFFICULT** HINTS, TURN TO PAGE **159**
FOR **MEDIUM** HINTS, TURN TO PAGE **169**
FOR **EASY** HINTS, TURN TO PAGE **179**
FOR **SOLUTIONS**, TURN TO PAGE **190**

Once I had ascended the tower, which I remembered from a map was called Readingum Abbey, I saw the area in full. A winding river ran from the north to the east, with a pig farm to the west. The rest of what I could see was England as I had never experienced, despite having lived there for most of my life. Not Alva's England, though. I was overwhelmed by the lush greens that were barely experienced in the height of summer and a spectrum of colours from the various plants untouched by motorways, pollution and industrialization. This hit home stronger than even Greece or Egypt had. Part of me imagined that I was on holiday elsewhere, but knowing that this really was England was an unmistakable reminder that I was in a completely different time.

A waterwheel that sat to the side of the abbey, slowly turning next to a huge stack of barrels, took my attention when a robed individual ran past. The movement of his running was enough to spark my interest and pull me away from my eagle-like vision of the area. I leaped down to a lower roof and dived into a cart that seemed conveniently placed below. On emerging, I darted into the building near the waterwheel to locate the runner.

"Please do not hurt me," he called out. He wore the robes of a monk.

The monk's presence was not surprising but I couldn't help but be suspicious. The possibility of a concealed

LUNDEN

EYE PATCH

WYCHAM

PET WOLF

weapon, or even a soldier having donned the robes, caused me to keep my guard up.

"What are you doing here?" I demanded.

"This is an abbey. I am a monk. All I do here is pray and make beer."

"Beer?"

"Please, take some," he pleaded, pointing at a barrel to his side. "The water comes fresh from the Holy Brook, which supplies the beer and powers the process. You will find none better in the county."

I looked up at the elaborate waterworks that had been constructed here. Nodding back, I called for the rest of my Vikings to assist me in transporting the barrel back to our homestead.

Eivor was waiting for me. I was their *Jomsviking* and, as long as I was paid, my loyalty and that of my group would not falter.

"It is good to see you, Alva," Eivor announced.

"You too, Eivor. Were you successful in your task?"

"Basim is insisting I locate more of these places, and I found something that may lead to one. I think you should take a look first. It is in London, marked on this map."

The map was well drawn but with strange instructions on how to access the location.

"They call it a Bureau, The Hidden Ones." Eivor continued. "And you, were you successful?"

I looked over my shoulder and flicked my head at the barrels being unloaded from the longboat.

Eivor smiled. "Tonight we feast."

My head was remarkably clear considering the volume of drinks I had imbibed the night before. Alva's body must have been more used to it than I was back in the 21st century. Dismounting my horse, I saw a large tower in the centre of some ruins.

Is the entrance truly inside? I thought. London – or Londinium, as my host knew it – was still a giant settlement, but nothing like the world I knew. I couldn't even tell where I was in relation to the river but following the map showed promise. I climbed up and looked over the tower's surrounding walls.

Indeed, there was water within but, before heading down toward it, I realized that

my entire surroundings had strange markings on the ground, painted, or arranged with rocks into an almost sundial-like image. The numbers stretched around the tower to leave a shadow. While the shadow may not have been important, I took note of the strange number order, then pushed myself off the thin ledge and gracefully dived into the cold water below. It seemed like forever swimming between the stone walls but, eventually, I came across an open chamber and more importantly, the chance to take a breath.

I climbed out and, dripping, walked toward a metal-grated doorway between two lit torches with a large, stylized "A" towering above them.

"Do not move," a shadowy figure commanded from behind me.

I felt a thin point of steel jabbing into my back and realized that I had very little choice but to obey.

"Who are you?" The figure asked.

"I am Alva. I was asked to find you by a man called Basim Ibn Ishaq. Well, my clan was."

The steel was removed and I gently turned around to see a familiar weapon.

"That blade. Is it from Baghdad?"

"This one? No. But we have many like it. Perhaps you are mistaken."

I could tell Alva was slightly surprised at the knowledge they had; mine cast back into their body, although, if I was wrong about the blade, why was I here in the 9th century?

"Clearly, you have knowledge of us."

"The Hidden Ones?" I dared.

"Indeed. And if you are looking for a specific one in this country, there is only one place that it is likely to be."

"And where is that?"

"In the hands of The Connection."

That name... was that not what Malcolm was calling himself, far into the future? *Surely, this couldn't be the same person.*

"Why are they called The Connection?"

"You have heard of him?" the figure asked. "The Order of the Ancients is our old enemy and they take many forms. Cults, groups, and he is a kind of... go-between. He collects branches of The Order as well as the blades of Hidden Ones that are killed."

"So how do I find him?"

"We cannot allow you to ruin all of the work

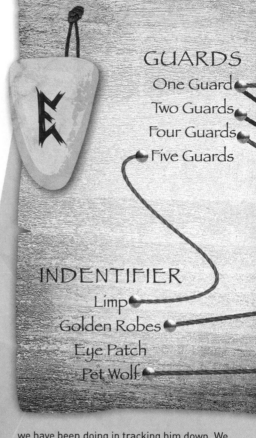

GUARDS
One Guard
Two Guards
Four Guards
Five Guards

INDENTIFIER
Limp
Golden Robes
Eye Patch
Pet Wolf

we have been doing in tracking him down. We need to kill him."

The figure nodded at the gate, which swung aside almost immediately. He waltzed into the book-filled room to see two more cloaked figures and waved his arm toward a wooden board raised up toward the side of the room. It had pieces of red and green string connecting various words.

"This is the information we have. Green string means that the words are connected – for example, we have just learned that The Connection has four guards."

74

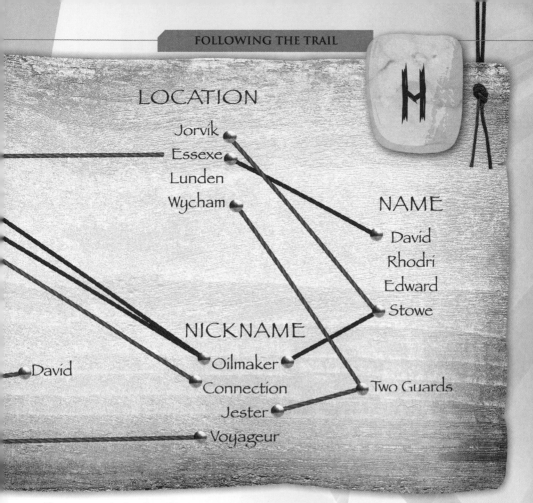

LOCATION

Jorvik
Essexe
Lunden
Wycham

NAME

David
Rhodri
Edward
Stowe

NICKNAME

David

Oilmaker
Connection
Jester
Voyageur

Two Guards

The man attached a piece of green string between "The Connection" and "Four guards".

He continued, "Red string means we know that it is incorrect – for example, we already know that The Oilmaker does not have one, two or three guards. Each potential option can only have one correct answer, and they do not share the answers with any other options. Can you tell me what we can now infer from our new information about The Connection?"

I looked at the board and realized that The Oilmaker now only had one option left.

"The Oilmaker has five guards?" I offered.

"Correct. Perhaps you will determine

information that can help us finish this board. We need five more strings on the board to be able to solve this. If you find two of these options elsewhere, such as 'The Connection – four guards', they will be correct. I hope that makes sense."

"I think so," I said and nodded nervously.

FOR **DIFFICULT** HINTS, TURN TO PAGE **159**
FOR **MEDIUM** HINTS, TURN TO PAGE **169**
FOR **EASY** HINTS, TURN TO PAGE **179**
FOR **SOLUTIONS**, TURN TO PAGE **190**

Before I could think any further, a booming voice echoed around the chamber.

"Hiding in the shadows suits you, vermin."

The four of us spun round to see a large, armoured foe, mocking us all from behind another gate. He waved his hand and six more guards approached carrying a battering ram.

"We are discovered. We must abandon this place," the shadowy figure announced.

"They're not with me," I insisted, getting ahead of any accusation.

The figure smiled, "Then you should prove it."

He threw a thin sword at me by the hilt, which I caught quickly and turned toward our enemies. Just one attempt was enough to throw the gate off its hinges and expose us. Instantly, The Hidden Ones launched toward the guards but the large one – a true Goliath – fixed his eyes upon me. I swiped at his head, which he swiftly sidestepped. Another swipe and he caught it with a metal bracer on his wrist, then lunged to grab hold of me. My reactions were trained and on top form, and I evaded to the side and plunged the sword straight through his back. I turned around to see that the others had also successfully taken out their foes.

Something about the pile of bodies, shining in different colours, seemed important, but I had a feeling I might not need to think about it yet. Presently, I had other things to distract me.

"It seems that we are discovered," the figure said to everyone. "We must leave this place at once."

I nodded, although I felt that his advice wasn't necessarily aimed at me.

"Good luck finding The Connection," he continued, this time facing me directly. "We must remove our most valuable records, save perhaps for something for those loyal to our cause to find us. There is, however, a document that you may find of use in the drawer in the cabinet behind you. Do, please, leave this place locked up before you leave." He patted me on my waist encouragingly.

I turned to see the cabinet in question and opened the drawer. It was a diagram of what looked like a compass, or code wheel or something. Letters were arranged around the outside in an unusual order. I had a quick scan of it but didn't see anything obvious hidden within the letters. Before I could ask any questions, I spun around to see that the others had all silently departed, having grabbed what they needed beforehand.

Looking back, Alva's natural instinct to check everything thoroughly paid off, as spinning the page over revealed a string of letters and numbers that just served to confuse me further.

K->B F = ?   E->P W = ?
U->B V = ?   O->L J = ?
C->J L = ?   E->B I = ?
S->Z W = ?   H->G R = ?
F->V W = ?   U->X H = ?
S->A L = ?   M->P Y = ?
C->G T = ?   S->N Q = ?

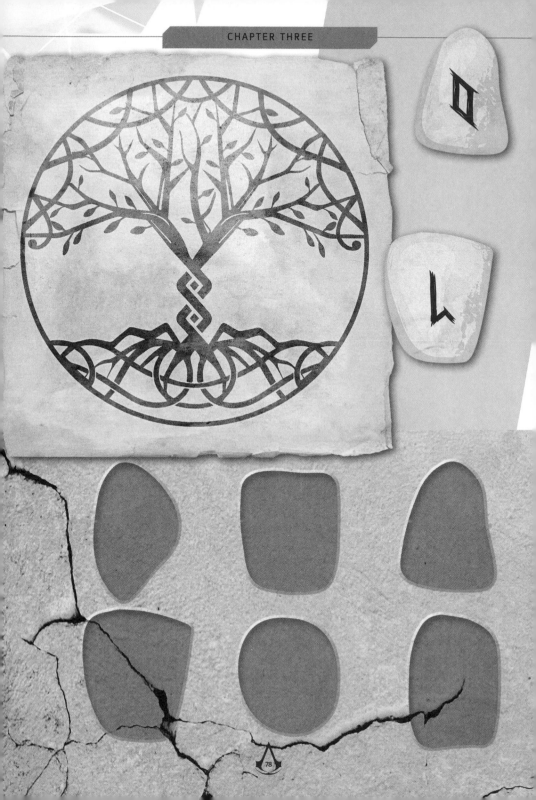

The figure had asked me to lock the bureau up, but I didn't know how, so I quickly investigated what was available to me.

The way I had come in was one route I couldn't do much more than closing the gate on, so I discovered the mechanism to do it and released the counterweight to slam it shut. The route our enemies had come in through was a broken stone wall, perhaps blown open by a nearby vase of oil or something similar. To close it, I would have to repeat the process around a weak point of the tunnel, and that was something I didn't want to get wrong. As I searched for anything that I could use, I spotted a small piece of fabric on the floor by a wall that seemed to be moving, blowing because of some unseen source. I scrabbled to the floor and saw a small gap in between the stones. I traced my sword over it, only

to find that the gap extended around the wall, drawing out the shape of a rune on it. While I was intending to be more careful, I couldn't stop Alva flinging the wooden table that was up against the wall across the room, papers and embers from a nearby torch dancing into the air.

The wall had a lot of these grooves and runes and, the more I stared at it, the clearer they became.

I kept staring until the words made sense. *Another clue to The Hidden Ones' board?* Suddenly, almost electronically, the runes began to glow. There was a deep rumble and the wall split in two, revealing another chamber that I recognized to be of Isu design. I was stuck fast – while I had seen this before, Alva was more terrified by them than I had ever felt. I pushed forward and looked for anything of note inside. A circular podium that I had seen before sprang into life. A man appeared this time, immediately addressing me.

"Spectator, I have learned of your visitations to our chamber. We do not have long," he began.

"What do you need to tell me?" Alva and I asked, more in synchronicity than I had felt previously.

"I am Vejovis. You must locate the blade."

I felt a little surprised that this advanced being was unaware of the mission I had already accepted.

"I believe it is in the hands of The Connection," I replied, pushing my words through Alva's lips enough for me to see myself in the simulation.

Vejovis smiled. "Then you are on the correct path. You must find my Sage."

"What is a Sage?" I asked.

I was ignored as he commanded, "Destroy this place, now that you have my message," he insisted, looking over at a large panel to the side of the circle. Without another word, his form disappeared and, in the blink of an eye, I was Alva once more.

I seemed to know what to do, and simply touching the panel caused a bar on the right of it to appear and slowly shrink in size. It was a countdown. Alva knew too and moved us back into the Bureau and out of the tunnel made by the visitors whose bodies littered the floor. My feet seemed to find the right spaces on the floor to avoid weapons, debris and anything else that would slow me down. I emerged into the sunlight, which felt brighter than reality because of the dark dungeon environment I had been immersed in, and the floor started rumbling. I was flung to the ground, with ringing in my ears as a side effect of whatever technology had collapsed the passage behind me. I figured the Isu vault had been sealed, though perhaps now the bureau was abandoned, someone else could still enter the original way, even though they wouldn't have anyone to let them through the gate – a problem for them.

For a second, I relaxed, until I felt a strange bulge on my waist where the figure had tapped me. I reached inside my jacket to find a page that had been planted there. It was a letter from someone calling themselves The Connection, describing a meeting in London at a specific time and place. This was my way of finding them. I had to be at that meeting.

Having such an advantage allowed me to be incredibly prepared. The Connection would be below a clocktower at a market stand and I was waiting above, perched on a ledge like an eagle waiting for my prey. I hadn't been given the information by The Hidden Ones without an understanding. If I was to find him, I must take this opportunity to assassinate him. I tried to focus and block out all of the noise of the simulation; birds flying around and normal denizens of the city weren't part of my objective. I took a deep breath and registered a man that seemed to stand out. I opened my eyes wider to see him brighten with a golden glow. He was surrounded by mercenaries. He must be The Connection. I held my bearded axe in my hand, poised for him to move within range underneath me and, without thinking about it, let Alva make her move. I sailed through the air and swung my axe as I reached the man, and cleanly took off his head, which soared upwards. Everything seemed to slow to a standstill as I used his body as a cushion for my landing. I looked up to see his face, spinning past me, almost grinning with a hidden knowledge. It slowed further and, right at the point of his eyes locking with mine, the rest of the simulation erupted into a polygonal mess. The remainder of his body returned to stand above me as I crouched onto the floor of this void.

"I am glad it was you," he said.

"Me? You know who I am?" Alva asked.

"My time is up. Now it is yours. I expect you want to know where the blade is," The Connection asked rhetorically. I hope you are listening carefully."

"Why do you act like your death is your desire?"

"It is a matter of time. But not the end."

"Do you not hold the web of The Order together?"

"For now. But an inevitable setback is still just a setback. I will see you again."

The words sent a shiver down my spine. I reached out through Alva to whisper a name.

"Malcolm?"

His look was that of confusion. Perhaps I had misjudged. I was growing tired of killing people that seemed to leave the experience happier than me.

"We will see. I suppose you would like the blade's location." He began to disintegrate but, before he had evaporated, called out some final words.

"My name – 4, my location – 3, my nickname – 9, my identifier – 5, my number of guards – 4."

That was it. An empty void and I had not returned.

> **! SOLVE TO PASS**
>
> **Once I knew where the blade was, I knew I could proceed.**

"Syria. The blade has moved to Syria," I announced, barely realizing I was back in my own body in the present day.

"Great job, Joey," Colm said warmly.

"Do you know who Vejovis is?" I asked.

"We have no records of an Isu called Vejovis."

"There is 'V'," Alera corrected. "Could that be Vejovis?"

"Potentially."

"Vejovis wants us to get the blade."

Colm moved closer to me and spoke in an almost whisper as Alera continued shutting down the systems around the Animus.

"Vejovis is not to be trusted," he started. "He is an Isu and their objectives are far beyond what we can understand. They have had millennia to plan and cultivate the right circumstances to make us do exactly what they want."

"I don't understand. Are they alive? Now?" I asked.

"What we know is that they were incredibly advanced but their entire civilization was destroyed. Individuals, however, have put things in place to try to revive themselves and, from what I gather, this may not be a good thing for humanity. A lot of them have no interest in preserving us – only themselves – and they will do whatever they have to do to return."

"You say a lot of them—"

"Some have proven to be benevolent but, frankly, it's not worth the risk unless there is more at stake. What about your vision at the start – that Malcolm character. Did you recognize him?"

"Are you asking if Vejovis is Malcolm? No, they're different people," I assured Colm.

"From how they looked, or who they were?"

"I don't understand."

Colm nodded and stayed silent for a few moments. I took the opportunity to stand up from the Animus and gather my equilibrium. Alera broke the quiet.

"Get some rest. Syria is a fantastic lead and one that seems to check out. We'll tell you the plan in the morning."

"Why not tell me the plan until then? I'm raring to go."

"Because we don't have one yet," Colm finished.

I nodded, skipped up a couple of stairs by the Animus and headed toward the exit, where I saw a familiar face.

"See you tomorrow, Eivor," I called out.

"You will," Eivor replied, and I did not even think twice about the tricks my mind was playing on me.

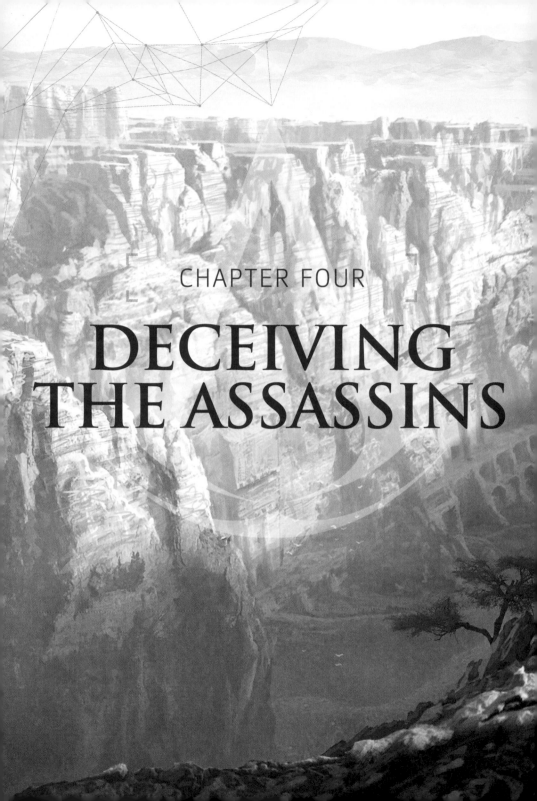

CHAPTER FOUR

DECEIVING THE ASSASSINS

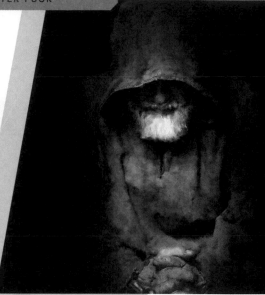

I entered the Animus chamber the next morning after what was a disturbed but still useful sleep. Alera and Colm were already there, whispering about the night before.

"So, I should probably explain ..." I started.

"No need. The mind can play tricks on you when you're back and forth into the Animus," Alera reassured. "It's like waking from a vivid dream. It takes a moment to become completely aware of where you are."

I nodded, only half-believing her. Colm stayed silent. He knew otherwise and I could sense it.

"Well, no time to lose, I guess," he announced. "I have spent the night delving into the historical record of Alva and their links to Syria. There was a slim window of time where the owner of the blade is likely to have been, and The Hidden Ones became The Assassin Brotherhood that we know today. In twelfth-century Damascus, The Order of the Ancients had become the Templars, and the Syrian blade collection had been moved to a place known as 'The Hideout'."

"So, you're sending me to Damascus?"

"Not exactly ..." started Alera nervously. "We have no specific link to Damascus that we can just send you to directly. You'll find yourself in a castle fortress called Masyaf, among the other Assassins. Whatever happens, you must ignore their instructions and go to Damascus. The Templars want the blade but you must reach The Hideout first. It is your priority. You need to help whomever you find there."

"How can I change what my host does so drastically?" I asked.

"If things go to plan, you will not have to," she replied cryptically.

"And to defy the Assassins, surely that is crossing a line."

I looked between them and sighed; I realized that I would not get any further information and sat on the Animus once more, filled with anticipation for the simulation to begin.

The piercing eyes of a wizened man with a long, grey beard and black cloak looked directly at me. Well, the piercing eye. One of them was cloudy and of no use to the man.

"Faisal," he began, revealing who I was. "Do you know your mission?"

"Of course, Master: to flank the oncoming forces and cause panic, driving them from our home."

I looked around and noticed that we were on a large balcony, or battlement, of a castle. This fortress at the top of a mountain and its village down the path was called Masyaf and was the home of the Assassins. Al Mualim, or "The Mentor", was the man in front of me, commanding the oncoming defence and a couple of other Assassins were nearby.

The Templars were sieging Masyaf.

"Remember, nothing is true, everything is permitted. Go now," he finished, and I did.

I was wearing a white hooded cloak with a red stripe down the middle and it flowed as I ran to my master's right, down a route that was hidden by the nearby walls across a giant chasm and rickety-looking planks of wood I had to hop across.

Another Assassin, Rafee, called out to me as I descended.

"Faisal, do you need help?"

"No," I insisted, intent on departing to Damascus as I had been instructed.

I saw his hand, a finger missing where his hidden blade would shoot out. I looked down at my own hand. I had the same injury. This was life for the Assassins at this time. I continued down the planks, away from the rest of the

Assassins. Occasionally, I could see back up to the fortress and hear Al Mualim shouting at the enemies below. I saw three men leap from the highest point of the fortress and land out of sight, part of the plans that were underway to defend this place. My focus was to protect the villagers, yet I couldn't stop thinking about my instructions: to defy my orders and head straight to Damascus.

I reached the outskirts of the village and saw a plethora of soldiers wearing the red cross that was so familiar to Faisal. I had to get to the entrance; wooden gates that I could sneak by if I was to leave this place and, ideally, without being seen. There were so many people coming and going that I couldn't risk assassinating any of the soldiers or trying to sneak past any route where they were standing. But I needed to get to the entrance.

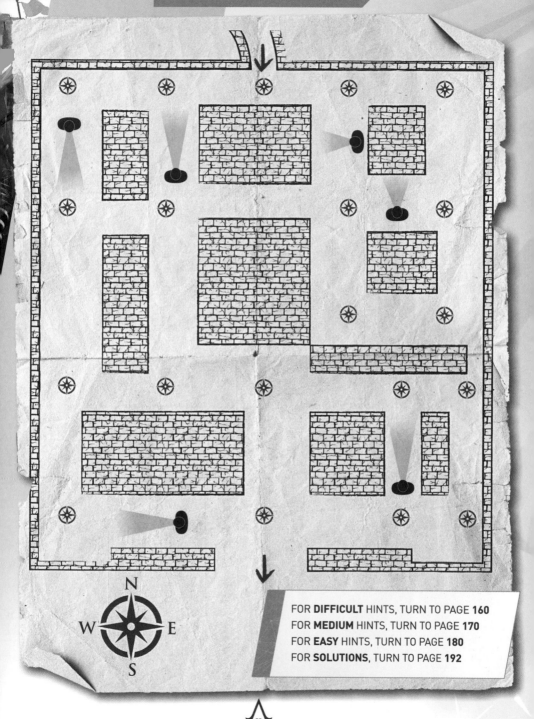

FOR **DIFFICULT** HINTS, TURN TO PAGE **160**
FOR **MEDIUM** HINTS, TURN TO PAGE **170**
FOR **EASY** HINTS, TURN TO PAGE **180**
FOR **SOLUTIONS**, TURN TO PAGE **192**

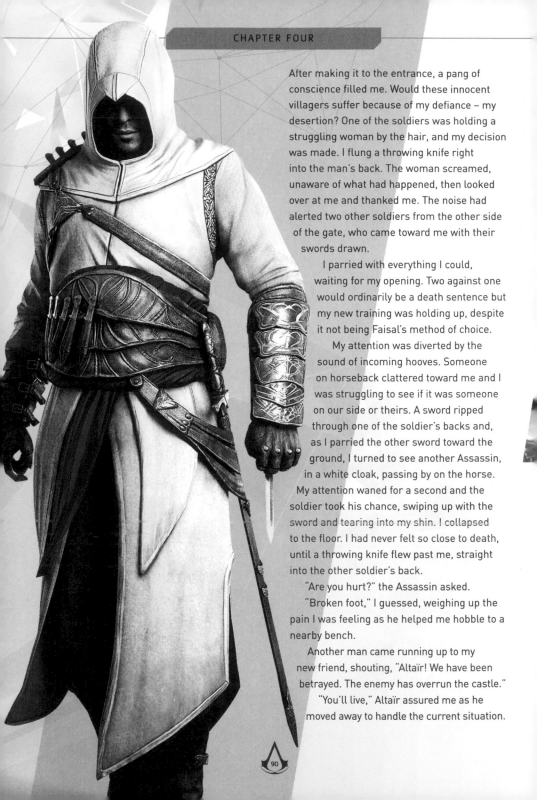

After making it to the entrance, a pang of conscience filled me. Would these innocent villagers suffer because of my defiance – my desertion? One of the soldiers was holding a struggling woman by the hair, and my decision was made. I flung a throwing knife right into the man's back. The woman screamed, unaware of what had happened, then looked over at me and thanked me. The noise had alerted two other soldiers from the other side of the gate, who came toward me with their swords drawn.

I parried with everything I could, waiting for my opening. Two against one would ordinarily be a death sentence but my new training was holding up, despite it not being Faisal's method of choice.

My attention was diverted by the sound of incoming hooves. Someone on horseback clattered toward me and I was struggling to see if it was someone on our side or theirs. A sword ripped through one of the soldier's backs and, as I parried the other sword toward the ground, I turned to see another Assassin, in a white cloak, passing by on the horse. My attention waned for a second and the soldier took his chance, swiping up with the sword and tearing into my shin. I collapsed to the floor. I had never felt so close to death, until a throwing knife flew past me, straight into the other soldier's back.

"Are you hurt?" the Assassin asked.

"Broken foot," I guessed, weighing up the pain I was feeling as he helped me hobble to a nearby bench.

Another man came running up to my new friend, shouting, "Altaïr! We have been betrayed. The enemy has overrun the castle."

"You'll live," Altaïr assured me as he moved away to handle the current situation.

I was a little shellshocked and my new injury giving me some serious limitations. Altaïr had left his horse, and I realized that this may be my last chance to depart for Damascus, any guilt for leaving Masyaf lost because of my own inability to help defend the castle. I hopped over and hoisted myself onto the horse, grabbing the reins and turning it toward the gate. I pressed my feet into the horse's flank and sped up to a gallop – riding was clearly now a new skill of mine.

Before long, I had gained enough distance from Masyaf to be confident that I was not in danger from the conflict. I slowed my horse and took a moment to recover. I jumped off, landing on my good foot, and removed the boot and enough clothing to see the damage that had been inflicted on me. It seemed that my foot was undamaged, but the sword had sliced quite deeply into the muscle above it, which would certainly affect the rest of my mission. I wrapped the material I had removed around the leg as tightly as possible to reduce the bleeding and, once I was confident that moving wouldn't affect it, I got back on the horse and continued, slower than before, to find somewhere for the horse to drink before my longer voyage to Damascus. I knew of a small

DISTANCE ARMY CAN TRAVEL BEFORE NEEDING RESUPPLY

MASYAF

stream that emerged briefly at a covered point in a rock face but, upon arrival, I came across two Templar soldiers. Not wanting to cause an issue, I decided that waiting for them to leave would be the best move. They were filling huge pots with water and loading them onto a horse-drawn carriage. After consulting a map, they headed off, back toward the desert. I brought my horse forward for a quick drink, then followed the Templars to their next stop: an empty hole by a small tree.

The men were burying water along the route to Damascus to allow further Templar forces to replenish themselves along the route.

The map must show where they're all buried, I thought. If I could get hold of that map and somehow sabotage the system, I could do some good for the Assassins on my way. Perhaps this will redeem me for my disobedience.

It was not ideal, but I had some throwing

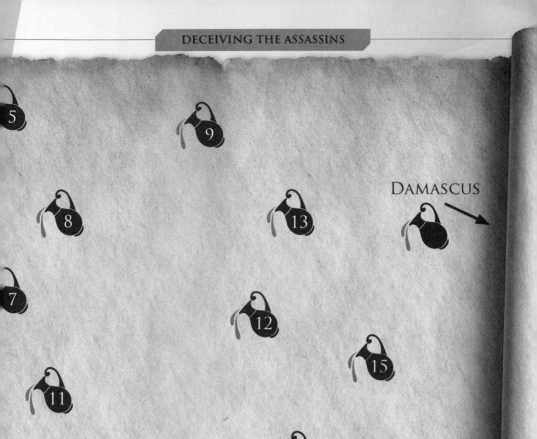

DAMASCUS

knives left and could easily take the soldiers out from a distance.

Once I had despatched them, I smashed the pot of water they'd buried and took a look at the map to see the routes and placements of the water and supplies.

I didn't have a lot of time but if I could figure out a way of reaching one more of these pots and destroying it to break the chain, it would be a huge help. Other soldiers would

either not arrive at all or make it to Masyaf tired and unable to stand up against the force of the Assassins.

FOR **DIFFICULT** HINTS, TURN TO PAGE **160**
FOR **MEDIUM** HINTS, TURN TO PAGE **170**
FOR **EASY** HINTS, TURN TO PAGE **180**
FOR **SOLUTIONS**, TURN TO PAGE **193**

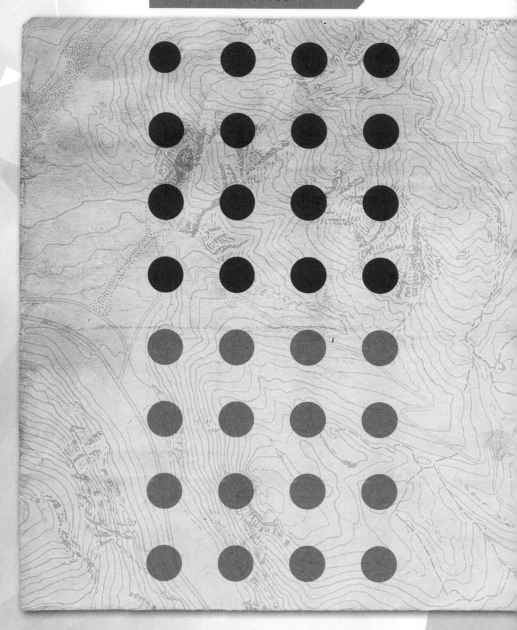

I was proud of myself for the manoeuvre but spotted markings on the other side of the map. They were a plan for a full army that would be marching that way. I couldn't understand it all yet, but it was bound to be important. Using the layout, I would be able to avoid any further

FOR **DIFFICULT** HINTS, TURN TO PAGE **160**
FOR **MEDIUM** HINTS, TURN TO PAGE **170**
FOR **EASY** HINTS, TURN TO PAGE **180**
FOR **SOLUTIONS**, TURN TO PAGE **193**

conflict, but I still had quite a way to go and I still did not know the route to The Hideout or what would be contained within.

The path to Damascus was surprisingly uneventful but it gave me the opportunity to breathe in this new experience, time and place. Information came to me as I simply thought about it, like the fact that it was 1189 AD and my creed as an Assassin. Was this really what Colm and Alera were a part of?

My horse emerged from a thin passageway between rocks to a wide vista that gave me a powerfully moving view of my objective. The spires and white walls of Damascus caused my jaw to drop. Even though Faisal had seen it before, he clearly enjoyed the sight and was both confused and yet relieved to have reached my objective. He didn't seem to be fighting what I was doing, almost as if this had been his intention all along.

The market stalls lining the entrance sold all manner of things that on another day I would have been thrilled to explore. Instead, I dismounted my horse, almost forgetting my injury, and saw a row of guards blocking my way. I spotted a small group of similarly white-robed individuals with their hands together as if they were praying. Scholars moved freely in and out of the city and, by walking with them, trying to mask my limp and keeping my head down, I passed them without issue. As soon as I was out of view, I slunk into the shadows and realized that I was searching for a place in a city that I didn't know, with no idea of how to find it. My first objective needed to be to get a good view of the surrounding area, just in case I could remember anything that Faisal knew. There was a large spire nearby and I approached it nervously. Being able to climb it with a damaged limb would be possible but not as easy a task as I had grown used to.

I realized that I would need to take multiple moments to get my breath on the way up. I estimated I could move four places before having to stop, but only certain holds were placed in a good enough position to be able to rest. As long as I took a route that would lead to one of those rest spots every four holds or less, I could make it to the top. I could also jump over one broken handhold, but only if I moved immediately to a rest spot.

FOR **DIFFICULT** HINTS, TURN TO PAGE **160**
FOR **MEDIUM** HINTS, TURN TO PAGE **170**
FOR **EASY** HINTS, TURN TO PAGE **180**
FOR **SOLUTIONS**, TURN TO PAGE **194**

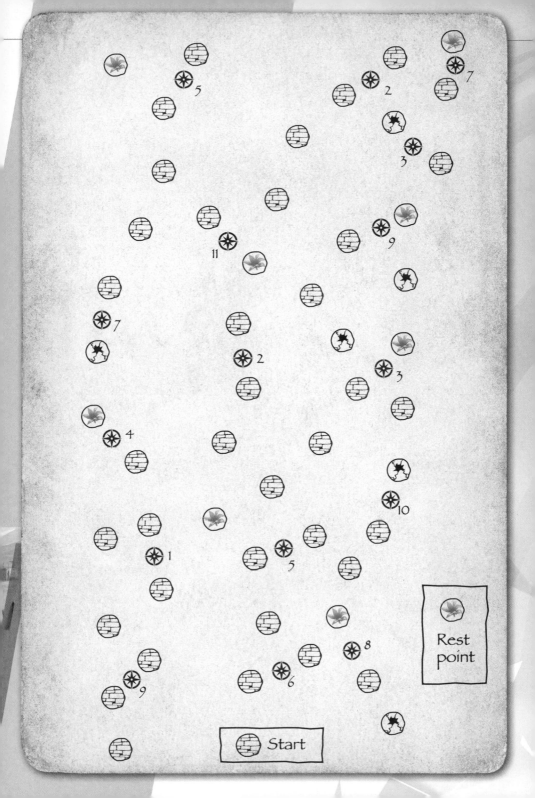

It was a struggle but I made it. Suddenly, though, my relief was overtaken by a feeling of panic as I quickly glanced below me to make sure I wouldn't have to climb back down. A huge pile of leaves looked like it might soften my landing, so I breathed a sigh of relief.

Looking back up, I admired the vista, only to nearly fall off the peak as the simulation seemed to glitch once more. Was there something different about the view now?

FOR **DIFFICULT** HINTS, TURN TO PAGE **160**
FOR **MEDIUM** HINTS, TURN TO PAGE **170**
FOR **EASY** HINTS, TURN TO PAGE **180**
FOR **SOLUTIONS**, TURN TO PAGE **195**

I was starting to feel a little lightheaded, either from my leg or the glitching, but Faisal had already made the decision to jump down and I sailed past my original climb, down to the leaves, which exploded out from under me as I landed. It was a harder landing than I had hoped for but I was still able to continue on my way. I headed toward the point where some of the glitches had happened to see a flickering set of glyphs that looked like it was related to the previous ones, in a grid-like format. I sketched out a quick map of the area of the city that I was in, but my mind was playing

tricks on me and I could see numbers by some of the points of interest, as if my knowledge – or Faisal's – was being documented and identified by the Animus. *One of those locations might be home to The Hideout,* I thought.

A spire to the left of my map stood out to me, the numbers confirming that I was on the correct path and heading toward The Hideout. I wondered what I'd find there: a stash including the blade I had been searching the world through time to find, or someone hiding there that I needed to protect?

I made my way through the streets,

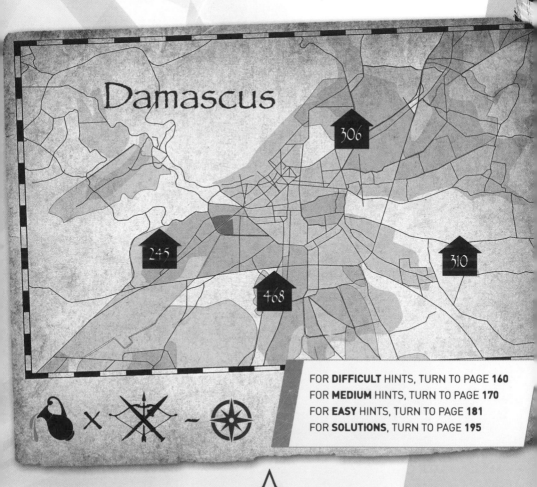

FOR **DIFFICULT** HINTS, TURN TO PAGE **160**
FOR **MEDIUM** HINTS, TURN TO PAGE **170**
FOR **EASY** HINTS, TURN TO PAGE **181**
FOR **SOLUTIONS**, TURN TO PAGE **195**

gently pushing the crowds out of the way as I silently approached; I had never felt so like an Assassin as on my stealthy path through the guard-filled Damascus. A couple of times I spotted a more heavily armoured soldier sporting a large red cross on their chest; they must be our enemies from The Order of the Templars, but now was not the time to approach. I looked around to see where one of them was going, only to turn back and come face to face with two that had turned down the thin passageway I was moving through. I panicked. Turning around would be suspicious, yet my camouflage would only deceive them from afar. I scanned the immediate area and saw a woman sitting on a nearby bench. I decided that they had passed. Blending in next to the woman seemed to work as the two Templars approached, but my heartbeat was so loud and fast that I was sure it would

give me away. They were right next to me now and I prayed that I wouldn't have to fight; my wounded body would not stand up to attack. Stealth was my only option.

One of the men shoved a pedestrian, who fell by my feet. I gently offered my hand to help him up, and cautiously lifted him onto the bench. He thanked me and, as much as I was trying to keep my head down, I couldn't help but raise it to catch a glimpse of the Templar that had pushed him. He caught my eye and, for a moment, I thought I'd been rumbled.

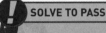

SOLVE TO PASS

When I knew which location the Animus was pointing me toward, I knew I could proceed.

He held my gaze a little too long and, just when I thought he was going to announce my presence, he lunged toward me threateningly. He stopped just before reaching me, expecting me to flinch, but I did not and, despite his clear annoyance, he and his companion continued down the street. I breathed a sigh of relief and found myself shaking. My nerves, rather than Faisal's.

I hopped up and continued on my path but, just as I ducked into another street, I caught a glimpse of the Templars turning around in suspicion. But it was too late – I was gone.

I reached the spire and looked at its entrance. Was this The Hideout, I wondered? The decision of whether to knock or just enter was out of my hands, as Faisal pushed the door open and came face to face with a large Templar soldier. A moment of nerves gave way to my quick thinking.

"My apologies. I must be in the wrong place," I gently spoke under my breath, while bowing my way back outside.

"It depends if you are looking for The Hideout or not," replied the Templar.

I was confused. Why would a Templar, who could clearly see who I was, be willing to help me?

"I am," I admitted.

"Well, you've found him."

"Him?"

"You thought The Hideout was a place. No, it is a person. It is me."

Of course, this fit the way the Templars have codenames. My instructions, however, were just to find The Hideout and help whoever was inside in order to locate the blade.

"Do you know why you are here?" he asked cryptically.

"No," I replied, brevity being my best method of avoiding revealing my true intention.

"I have need of your assistance. I have a package that must be smuggled out of Syria."

This had to be the blade, and perhaps helping The Hideout would genuinely help our cause back in my time. Or maybe this wasn't a decision for me and was simply how things took place.

"Do I have a choice?" I asked.

"We always have a choice but, by walking in here, I believe you have already made yours," he answered, tossing the package at me.

I caught it and unwrapped the material to find the blade I had been looking for. I was in the right place. I quickly wrapped it up again, stuffed it into a satchel that was sitting on a ledge to one side and hung the satchel around my neck.

"I need you to head to Beirut and ship the blade out to a safe place. I have a contact in the stables outside the city who will find you once you arrive and take you there."

Before I could reply, the door behind me opened to reveal a familiar face: Rafee, the Assassin who had offered his help in Masyaf.

"Faisal, what are you doing here, with a Templar?"

I span around to see The Hideout ducking behind a curtain, where he pulled a fake wall closed, the door sealing behind him.

"Rafee, it's not what it looks like."

"You know the Creed. You know what I have to do."

I had to act, and I couldn't think of an alternative. Nothing is True, Everything is Permitted. To complete my mission in modern times, I had to ensure Faisal completed his. I had to kill Rafee before he killed me. I glanced quickly around the room to determine my best option. I was clearly at a disadvantage because of my injuries and my mind was fragmented.

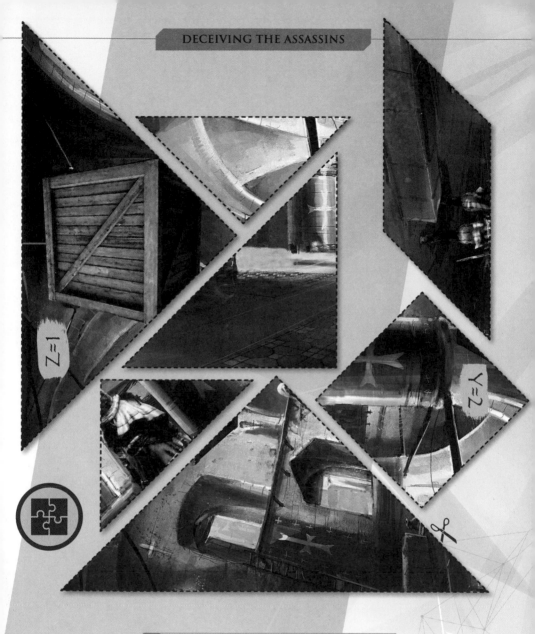

Z=1

Y=2

FOR **DIFFICULT** HINTS, TURN TO PAGE **160**
FOR **MEDIUM** HINTS, TURN TO PAGE **170**
FOR **EASY** HINTS, TURN TO PAGE **181**
FOR **SOLUTIONS**, TURN TO PAGE **195**

It seemed worse to be betraying my own, even if the greater mission was still on target, but I sliced the rope next to me, which dropped the crate onto Rafee's head. He collapsed onto the floor and I took the opportunity to leap over him. Looking into his's eyes as I plunged my own blade into his chest was one of the most intimate moments I had experienced within the Animus. My own hidden blade meant that my hand was resting around the wound and I could feel the blood trickle between my fingers. Rafee was calm and I was expecting him to look angrier than he did. He took a quick breath – the only noise he made – and the world disintegrated around us. I looked around to see everything recede, and then back down to my bloodstained hands, but Rafee was no longer there. He was pacing around a few feet away from me in the grey void, searching for what to say to me. Eventually, he turned to me.

"Why would you betray us?"

"Is it not possible that both of us are fighting for the same thing?" I argued.

"I forgive you."

"You do?"

"Everything is Permitted. I have known you for a long time. Perhaps my death is necessary for our cause."

I was shocked at how easily Rafee was willing to accept his own death. Of course, this wasn't exactly Rafee. My previous assassinations had left me with a version of the target that was more knowing than their live versions would have been. Perhaps this understanding was a gift from Rafee that confirmed I was on the right path.

"I promise that I will not allow your death to mean nothing," I started. "What I am doing is for the Creed, and beyond the lives of you and I."

"See that you succeed then," he demanded, smiling at me.

With that, the form of his simulation dispersed into the void.

I raised my head to find myself back in the spire where The Hideout had met me. I spotted a Templar cloak on top of a barrel and saw the benefits of disguising myself to ease my departure from the city. I flung it on and left the room as quickly as possible. Retracing my steps back was a lot simpler than on the way there, as I had no one to avoid. Guards waved me through and other Templars nodded at me respectfully. It was a technique I should have considered previously but getting hold of the Templar clothing was not normally an easy task.

I made it outside the gates and found my horse. It was a relief to get off my feet. I had a long journey ahead of me, to Beirut. Just then, a shabbily dressed man swiftly approached me, fixated on my clothes.

"Are you The Hideout's contact?" he asked.

"I could ask the same question of you."

"Yes. Where do you need to go?"

I figured that this was a kind of test. If I knew the answer, I could have only got the information from The Hideout.

"Beirut," I confirmed.

"This is true."

"And from there? Where does the package need to rest?"

"We will pass it on to someone who will know when we get there."

"No. I cannot trust this with anyone else. I will take it all the way," I demanded.

"As you wish. We have far to travel. Bring your horse to feed. We will need it to be refreshed."

I followed the man to a small shelter that had some food within and a water trough for my horse. The water was mirky and worryingly unclean, yet still and full. By being dark enough to see nothing inside, it reflected the wall behind it effectively. It was a simple thing, yet suddenly brought my attention to the quality of the simulation. It was totally real and immersive, from the visuals to the sound of everything going on around me.

The man brought another horse to the water; the one he would be riding.

"Why is this package so important?" he queried.

"It will be important in the future," I answered.

The secrecy of The Order was starting to make sense. With each participant or worker being unaware of the full information, no one could learn enough to want to stop it. They were probably paid enough to not worry about it, though evidently not enough to avoid asking questions. Or perhaps this was all a test to see if I would share the information I had.

"Where is it meant to go after Beirut?" I continued.

"We will cross the sea and proceed to Constantinople."

"Istanbul?" I added, foolishly sharing its modern name.

"What are you talking about?" he rightfully asked.

"Oh, nothing. That is just what we call it where I come from."

"And where do you come from?" he probed.

I deliberately backed off, allowing Faisal to take more of a driver's seat. Had I made a mistake, or would this only be an issue to someone who was also aware of the future? Could multiple people be part of the same simulation?

"Far away from here," Faisal answered.

The horses had finished drinking and the water became still again. I walked over to take the reins and pull my horse away. As I leaned over the trough, I looked down into the mirrored water and saw a person I had met before. Perhaps "person" was the wrong word. I jumped backwards, shocked and confused, and looked up in horror toward the other man, who could not know the significance of what I had seen.

It was the face of Vejovis. Faisal looked exactly like Vejovis.

I lurched upwards out of the Animus, somehow forcing myself back into the brightness of present day.

"They're back," Alera announced.

"What happened? Did you instigate this?" Colm asked, rushing over to me.

"No. This was all Joey."

Colm looked at me and I looked back in a combination of confusion and disbelief.

"I saw Vejovis. The Isu. That was who I was," I screamed.

"That's not possible. Could it be a glitch? Systems bleeding over from one simulation to another?" asked Colm.

"No. That's not how it works. If Joey saw Vejovis, then Vejovis was there," Alera confirmed.

"How?"

"What if Faisal was a Sage?"

A Sage. That was the word Vejovis had spoken about back when I first met him.

"What is a Sage?" I pleaded, desperate for some understanding.

"A Sage is... kind of an incarnation of an Isu," Alera volunteered.

"The Isu still exist?"

"Not exactly," said Colm. "Think of it like an Isu trying to find a way to return and hiding their memories in the DNA of select humans in the hope that they will gradually bubble to the surface and influence humanity's behaviour enough to assist in their reincarnation."

I shook my head in disbelief. "So Faisal is a Sage? That means he looks like Vejovis?"

"Not exactly. But these are the genetic memories of people like Faisal. In theory, the simulation could have confused the genetics of him with that of the Isu to which he was a Sage," Alera suggested.

"This could be an unexpected advantage for us," Colm said.

"Of course," Alera replied. "It's kind of a bug in the Animus's simulation. If we can determine a Sage because of it, it gives us more information than a malevolent Isu may want us to know."

"Malcolm: is he a Sage?" I wondered aloud, starting to put things together.

Alera paused, as if I was yet to be fully trusted, before admitting their thoughts. "That is our best bet. Perhaps a Sage of Vejovis. His desire for both blades may not be just to control others. It may be the only way of bringing Vejovis back to life, fully."

"And that would be a bad thing?"

"That would be a bad thing," Colm confirmed. I nodded and stood up.

"I'm going to rest," I announced. It was met with no argument. "The blade went to Constantinople, by the way."

I had done my part and was already concerned that things were getting worse and worse. My leg was no longer injured but I still felt the injury from Masyaf, somehow. And when I looked down, I could swear I was missing a finger.

A HIDDEN TOMB

My dreams were filled with Assassins of the past: some that I had seen in the Animus and some that I couldn't have known about. Was I getting better at tuning in to these genetic memories, or were they getting better at infiltrating my brain? All I knew was that something was awakening in me and I couldn't decide whether or not I liked it just yet. I walked back into the Animus chamber confidently and decisively. Colm was nowhere to be seen but Alera greeted me surprisingly warmly.

"How did you sleep?"

"How do you think?" I replied defiantly. Alera's reaction made me rethink my words. "I'm sorry to be so..."

"Stressed? Overcome with feelings you don't understand? Someone else's feelings?"

"Something like that," I admitted.

"It's OK. The Animus tends to seep into your mind the more you use it."

"It feels like it."

"The Bleeding Effect," announced a voice from the entrance.

Colm had heard enough as he walked in.

"Colm," Alera warned sternly.

"Joey deserves to know," he insisted.

"Fine. You're experiencing what we call the Bleeding Effect."

"Sounds just wonderful," I joked dryly.

"The memories you are experiencing are... blending with your own," Colm explained. "It's how you are gaining more skills and abilities when outside the Animus. It's also why you've been seeing things and acting strangely." "You've noticed that?"

"We have," Alera confirmed.

"Why didn't you tell me? Is it permanent?"

"We assumed that, by keeping your journeys with each of your hosts relatively short, there would not be time to have this happen," said Colm. "If you had spent significant periods of time with Faisal or Khepri, for example, it would be almost expected, but what is happening here

is unprecedented in its speed."

"What do I do then?" I asked.

After a moment of silence, Alera took a few steps toward me.

"One way or another, we need to find this blade."

Colm interjected, "It was kept in the Hagia Sofia until the early thirteenth century when the place was plundered and the spoils were taken, in all likelihood, to Venice. There seem to be a lot of links to all of these times you've visited, almost like they are times of high Assassin activity, and we have one of those links to fifteenth-century Italy."

I paused, uncomfortable with the whole situation. "And after this?"

"We are getting closer to modern times. After this, preservation and records become clearer," Colm reassured me. "Your visit to Venice is likely the last thing we will need you for."

I nodded, half-relieved and half-concerned at the implication. Would their secrecy lead to friendship? Integration into the Assassin's brotherhood? Or would they discard me once they'd got what they needed from me? I felt my blood pumping and my newfound abilities tingling to be used. *If I have to, will I be able to kill these two?* I wondered.

The thought was easy to push aside. The Bleeding Effect was unexpected to them and, while they were certainly hiding some things from me, there was a fine line between allowing me to be aware of all of the information and overwhelming me.

"I'm ready. Let's get this over with."

"I hear Venice was nice at this time of year," Alera quipped jovially.

I sat down, glancing over at the two Assassins, and pushed down whatever it was inside me that was leading me to mistrust them. I didn't really have a choice, and at least they weren't the ones trying to kill me earlier. Just as I closed my eyes, I wondered if that would have been a good way of gaining my trust: setting

up a fake group of mercenaries to "save" me from. These weren't my thoughts. My paranoia was bubbling inside and I could tell that it was similar to what I'd felt on seeing those people that couldn't have been there earlier on. Was I going insane? My consciousness seemed to drift away from me, into the simulation world – my electronic dreams.

A crowd full of vitality emerged from the void, but it wasn't actually a crowd. It was individual people separated by walls growing out of simulation, which appeared a fraction of a second after the people came into view. Buildings, canals and bright sunlight swept a smile across my face and, just as I was looking into the distance, a door appeared right in front of me. It shocked me but made sense when I realized my arm was ahead of me in the air, balled into a fist. I was knocking on the door, my white cloak rolling off my wrist. Out of my periphery, I could see a white hood. I was clearly an Assassin.

The door opened to reveal a man in his thirties wearing what looked like a burgundy beret.

"Buongiorno. You must be Giulia," he guessed, correctly. "Ezio has told me you can be trusted."

Ezio? Giulia? My host's thoughts and memories were coming to me.

"Leonardo?" I said automatically.

"Yes, you have come to the right place."

It was Leonardo da Vinci. *The* Leonardo da Vinci. I was a little star-struck, partially because of his reputation, known by Giulia, and partially because of his legacy that I, Joey, knew from centuries later.

"Hold this and come in," he insisted.

I looked down at the item.

"What is this?"

Leonardo laughed as if I had made a joke.

"Is it not what you were expecting? Ezio asked me to make it and to give it to you. He said it should help you find what you are looking for, yes?"

I didn't know what I was looking for, or rather Giulia didn't. Of course, I needed that blade but I couldn't resist the chance to learn a little more about Da Vinci, although I had no idea what to say to him.

"It is a pleasure to meet you," I tried.

"And the same for me," he awkwardly replied. I couldn't decide if his awkwardness was because I was a woman or because I was acting strangely. "I know Ezio has been searching for something," he continued. "Is it the same as the object of your desires?"

"I don't know. Where has he been searching?"

"All over Venice. All over Italy, really, but you're in Venice now, so I assume it must be here."

"I am not from Venice. Can you show me around?" I asked, hoping for more of his time.

"I am busy, I'm afraid. Many commissions."

I looked around at various works of art in different states of completion. One took my eye: a sketch of the surroundings.

"That is not for someone else. It is my attempt to help Ezio with his search. These are the main places he has been. I wondered if there could be a pattern in his routes."

RIO DEL SERVI

● PARCO SAVORGNAN

RIO CA DOLCI

RIO MARIN

PONTE DI RIALTO ●   RIO DE SAN LEO

RIO AMALTEO   ARSENALE DI VENEZIA

BASILICA SAN MARCO ●

RIO DELLE MUNEGHETTE

FOR **DIFFICULT** HINTS, TURN TO PAGE **162**
FOR **MEDIUM** HINTS, TURN TO PAGE **172**
FOR **EASY** HINTS, TURN TO PAGE **182**
FOR **SOLUTIONS**, TURN TO PAGE **196**

"This is most useful, thank you," I started. "Where do you suggest I begin?"

"Your guess is as good as mine."

"I will leave you to your work," I said, sensing my welcome was running out.

Da Vinci walked me to the door and opened it for me. As I left, he wished me a good day and closed the door behind me. This was my opportunity to explore Venice and, hopefully, locate the item. Without much direction, I started walking, enjoying the environment. I came across an arched bridge and paused for a second to admire my surroundings, only to notice a man in white robes with a red cross.

The Templars were here as well. The man saw me and ran, which was unusual for a Templar, who would normally attack. It had to mean something. I crossed into a grassy square and looked for him but couldn't see where he had fled. Catching my breath, I focused on my surroundings and tried to block out the parts of it that couldn't be relevant, like a desaturation of the simulation. A red movement caught my eye and I looked up to see him peering out from behind a balcony, trying to avoid my vision. He ran into a building and slammed the door behind him. I explored it from all sides, climbing up to the balcony with ease. It was nice to have no injury again, but the door wouldn't budge.

Six figures emerged from the ground floor of the building. Something seemed suspicious about them, more so because the route had been blocked when I'd tried it. Each wore a mask – traditional Venetian masks that I recognized from their use in modern pop culture. Was there some significance to them that I needed to pay attention to?

I stopped for a moment, resigned to my failure in locating the Templar, but perhaps he had inadvertently led me to what I needed: an idea of where to find the item I was searching through time for. A combination of everything in my visit to Venice would lead me specifically to one place in the city.

SOLVE TO PASS

Once I knew where the item was hidden, I knew I could proceed.

FOR **DIFFICULT** HINTS, TURN TO PAGE **162**
FOR **MEDIUM** HINTS, TURN TO PAGE **172**
FOR **EASY** HINTS, TURN TO PAGE **182**
FOR **SOLUTIONS**, TURN TO PAGE **196**

The Basilica. I knew there were multiple places known as Basilica, but only one was on the map that Da Vinci had drawn – Basilica San Marco. I knew I had to head there, to the place I knew as Saint Mark's Basilica.

It wasn't hard to find, as grand in structure as it was meaningful to those with the Catholic faith. I ascended back to the top of the building I was next to and surveyed the rooftops. It took a second before I started running, jumping over canals and rivers, rolling to cushion my landings, and clambering up anywhere that was higher than the route I was running. I felt so free, more outside than I had ever felt before in the Animus. I could see the entire city and I felt like it was mine; everything was underneath me and my skills would allow me to stealthily view everything that happened below. I soared through the air, my stamina holding me up, far longer than in any of my previous incarnations, and I enjoyed the sense of power. When this was all over, I would find it hard to return to my normal life. Perhaps Colm and Alera would allow me to still use the Animus occasionally. It felt like an addiction now and, by my abilities seeping into my real life, I was growing from it.

Eventually, my thoughts left me as I saw the beautiful facade of the Basilica. In contrast to the blocky buildings and flat rooftops, this was all curves: arches, domes and artwork exposed for all to see. I saw the iconic "Horses of Saint Mark" above the entrance, which seemed somehow familiar to me but didn't especially stand out at the time.

I landed in the square in front of it and began to admire the design as I slowly approached, not wanting to give myself away to anyone that may think I was acting suspiciously and halt my progress. A crowd of people gathered in front and I slunk into the centre, moving between them effortlessly, like water through the cracks of the stone floor. It seemed like there were other Assassins in the crowd, wearing white, and I was able to pass by them quickly, jumping over them, almost without leaving a trail.

I pressed on to the entrance, walking toward the large gates that stopped anyone from walking in freely. Two guards stood in front of them, waving angry people away, who seemed frustrated at being refused entry.

These were Templars, and what they were doing inside must have been related to my objective. I looked up at a window above a balcony and saw that it was open. I needed to climb but doing so would give me away, so I would need to approach from another angle. The sun was to my left: the north side. To the south, it was shrouded in darkness. I remembered the order of colours I had seen at the base of the horses. Yellow, Red, Yellow, Blue, Blue, Green. The same colours of shirts that the crowd were wearing. That would be my route. I slid between people in the crowds and made my way to the corner of the Basilica, where I would not be seen, and heaved myself up quickly.

FOR **DIFFICULT** HINTS, TURN TO PAGE **162**
FOR **MEDIUM** HINTS, TURN TO PAGE **172**
FOR **EASY** HINTS, TURN TO PAGE **182**
FOR **SOLUTIONS**, TURN TO PAGE **198**

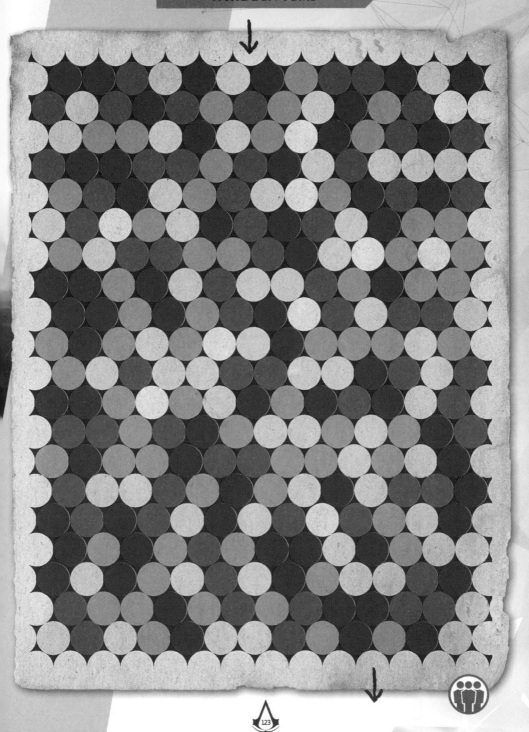

Ducking into the dimly lit main chamber, I swiftly and silently made my way to the rafters above. I could see someone below me: the Templar I had chased earlier. He was after the same thing as me and, while Giulia did not know the power of the item in question, I did. I wasn't sure anymore whether it was my host's or my own skills that allowed me to balance without fear. A misstep would see me plunging to my death below but, for now, I was fine. I took up position on the end of a wooden beam and saw the shadow it cast directly beneath me. Making my way down would take time but I wasn't worried. If I could land on top of the Templar – my target – his body would cushion my fall, but I needed to wait until he was right below me, in the shadow of the beam. He was wandering around, searching fruitlessly but methodically. My vision changed as I focused on his movement. Everything else lost colour but I could see the last seven moves he made.

Suddenly, it hit me that he was walking in a set path, repeating his actions over and over. Once he was underneath me, that would be his last step.

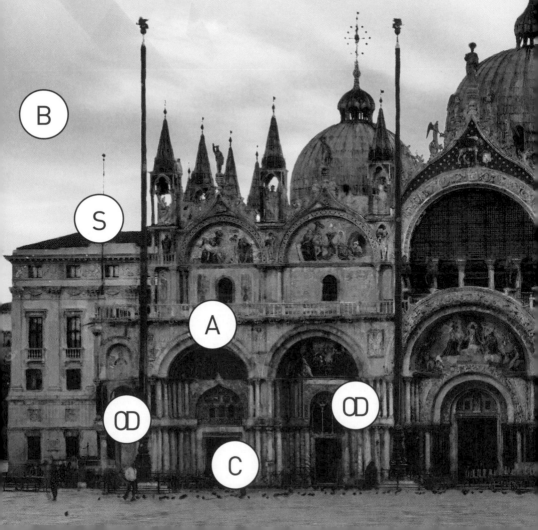

It was time. I was in position but my slight twinge of movement – anticipation mixed with excitement – made the slightest of sounds. It was enough for him to notice and he started to tilt his head up. I leaped off the wooden beam and plunged my hidden blade into his neck just as his eyes locked with mine. He showed no fear, just disappointment at having been beaten. He tried moving his limbs to thrust a weapon at me but he was already too far gone and his world melted around him, leaving us in our simulation void, with me still on the floor and him standing on a podium well out of range.

"Three down," he began. "So, you found me. Turn right. You must be proud. I have always evaded your kind previously."

"I wasn't searching for you," I admitted.

"You have heard of the treasure? One under. The hidden vault."

"Of course. It contains things that belong to our brotherhood."

"Property... Ownership is fleeting. Turn left twice. With every death comes transfer. I used to own my body. Now who does? Two down. Who decides what happens to it? If my wishes are honoured?"

"Your people stole our treasures. They were never yours."

"And you have stolen my life, yet you seem to think it was fit to take. Five left."

"Enough. I have nothing to learn from you."

"And maybe that is what you must learn. That not everyone must be listened to. Two down."

"My point is proven," Giulia replied smugly.

"And what about you, Spectator? Why do you speak to me?"

I froze. He was no longer talking to Giulia.

"Who am I?" he asked.

"You are a Templar."

"Not this form. Who am I?"

"Vejovis?" I ventured quietly.

"It is good to see you again. Three right, then repeat from the start."

"How are you here?"

"I am not where you think I am. I have found my way into your simulation but I must help you enter the vault, for that is where you will complete your destiny."

I was confused. Had he infiltrated the Animus somehow? Was this no longer a representation of the past, but instead, something this Isu being was creating?

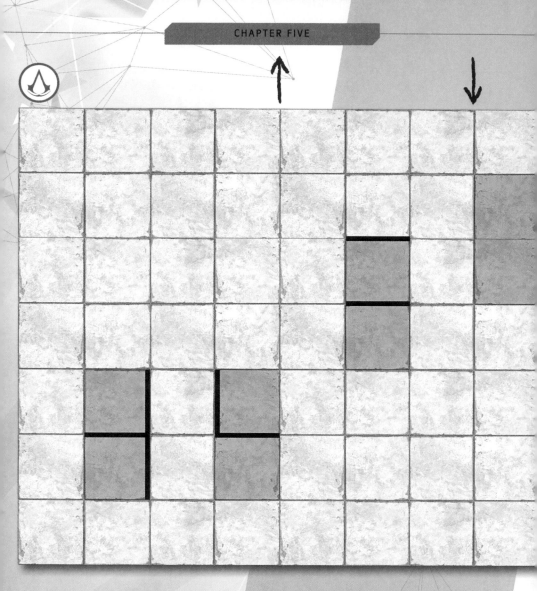

"You are losing synchronization. If you are unable to enter the vault, you will not find the information you seek."

"Then tell me how," I asked belligerently.

"I already have. Things are just beneath the surface," he whispered and then faded into smoke as the world reconstructed itself around me.

FOR **DIFFICULT** HINTS, TURN TO PAGE **162**
FOR **MEDIUM** HINTS, TURN TO PAGE **172**
FOR **EASY** HINTS, TURN TO PAGE **182**
FOR **SOLUTIONS**, TURN TO PAGE **199**

The Templar had not found the correct place but Vejovis's route sent me around the room until I found an even darker section of the chamber, where a tapestry hung in front of me.

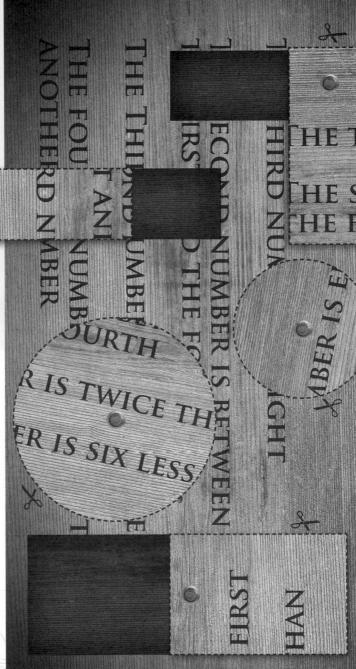

It was complicated and my first inclination was that, if it was important, it held a lot of information. I paused, thinking of Vejovis's last words and, in a moment of exploratory completionism, lifted the tapestry.

Text of some kind was scrawled underneath, with stones and rocks that stuck out. I reached out and touched them. Some of them moved back and forth within their grooves, while the circular ones were able to spin. I had to find the right combination to read the message, which did not take me long.

The message gave me a strange set of instructions but, upon slotting them in place, the wall seemed to judder and push inward. As it opened into a thin passageway, I knew I had found the vault. It reminded me of the tomb back in Ancient Egypt. Blue, metallic walls and smooth formations that were likely Isu in origin guided me down to a larger chamber underneath the city. I could hardly believe my eyes, that something so incredible existed so close to the reach of so many people, yet entirely undiscovered for centuries – possibly millennia.

Ahead of me was another podium, like the one in the first Isu chamber. Above the podium was a beam of light and, before I could do anything, it came to life, Vejovis appearing in front of me, as before.

"What is this? Who are you?" Giulia demanded, as fearfully as I had ever felt her.

"I am Vejovis. If this is a message for you, then you will know it," he said cryptically.

Almost instantly, a hologram of symbols and data flashed up and I knew it was a clue to the correct information that I needed.

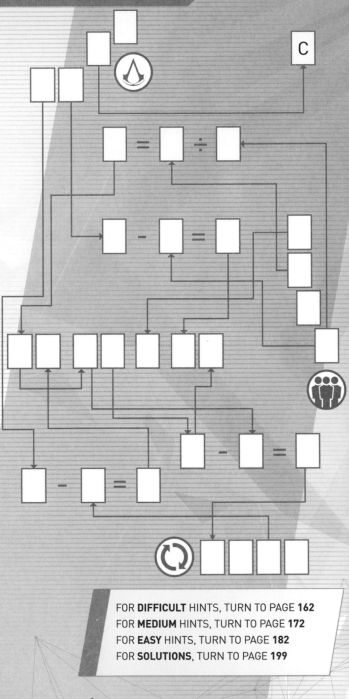

FOR **DIFFICULT** HINTS, TURN TO PAGE **162**
FOR **MEDIUM** HINTS, TURN TO PAGE **172**
FOR **EASY** HINTS, TURN TO PAGE **182**
FOR **SOLUTIONS**, TURN TO PAGE **199**

"Vejovis? I'm here. Joey is here," Giulia uttered, not truly understanding what I had made her say.

"My friend. I did not know when you would arrive, but I still have a long time to wait to see you in person," he replied warmly.

"Why am I here?"

"To hide this better than the fools who sacked Constantinople did."

He waved his arm to reveal the blade. The other half of the dagger back in my time. Giulia took it and I immediately felt a stronger connection.

"Where do I hide it?"

"Deeper within this chamber. Then it will be safe until the Spectator can make it here."

Giulia nodded, perhaps without understanding, but certainly with confidence

that she was doing the right thing.

"Use this to proceed further," he announced, pointing at a panel on the wall, which self-illuminated.

Giulia got closer, fearless of the technology that she had never seen but, before I could see any details, the simulation began to crumble and Vejovis called out,

"See you soon, Spectator."

I awoke with a start and turned to Colm.

"The blade, I think it's still in Venice. Saint Mark's Basilica."

He looked down at me protectively.

This was it. I knew where I had to go.

CHAPTER SIX

STOPPING THE CULT

I hopped off the Animus with a spring in my step. This was it. Colm had gone to find a laptop in order to book our flights to Venice, and I was left trying to think of what I had experienced. My incarnations flashed before me, not as a memory, but as something more physical. The Bleeding Effect, they had called it, and I hoped it would not last long. Pyramids, statues, Vikings and so much more were now part of me. I closed my eyes and held them tightly shut, trying to focus on the imagery, rather than let it wash over what was going on in real life. There was something about these simulations that wasn't right.

A longboat soared past me. The faces of those I had killed. I had killed all these people – it wasn't a simulation to me, or to those I had inhabited. I opened my eyes to see Alera in front of me, holding a gun to my forehead.

"They are coming," she announced.

"The Templars?" I asked, holding my cool a lot better than I expected in the circumstances.

"Yes."

"And you're just planning on holding me here until then?"

"You're on the wrong side. I don't know why you went along with what we asked of you, knowing what you know, but it's over."

I was starting to squirm. *Alera has been working with the enemy this whole time? Then they already know where the blade is. She must have told them straight away.*

I saw her finger start to squeeze the trigger and awaited the end.

A crash flew past my eyes. A hard drive, or some kind of computer equipment, smashed Alera in the temple and I turned my head to see Colm standing by the entrance. Taking my chance, I lashed out at Alera and, in a move that I could have only learned from my past, spun around, striking her with my foot in a roundhouse kick that wouldn't have looked out of place in the movies.

Colm rushed over to me. "What did she say?"

"The Templars are coming."

"I see. She was working for them," he said, almost as a confirmation of what he already knew.

"You suspected her?"

"The stakes are too high. Either side would be willing to do anything to get their hands on the blade, and you must have noticed the number of times she left almost immediately after

your sessions in the Animus. She was probably informing our enemy of what we'd learned."

"So, if they know where we're going, we can't waste any time, right?"

"Exactly." Colm nodded. "We need to get to Venice as soon as possible. The next direct flight isn't until tomorrow, so we're going to need to take an indirect route. It won't take us long to get to Heathrow Airport. With my contacts, we can get there and through security within an hour. Any flight in sixty minutes time or later is viable. We can transfer between flights at any airport in pretty much exactly thirty minutes."

I looked down at my watch. Time seemed to have lost all meaning after time within the Animus. It was 10.35 am. I peered over the laptop and opened a web browser to find flights.

"There's no time," Colm insisted. "I'll drive. You plan a route on the way."

FOR **DIFFICULT** HINTS, TURN TO PAGE **163**
FOR **MEDIUM** HINTS, TURN TO PAGE **173**
FOR **EASY** HINTS, TURN TO PAGE **183**
FOR **SOLUTIONS**, TURN TO PAGE **200**

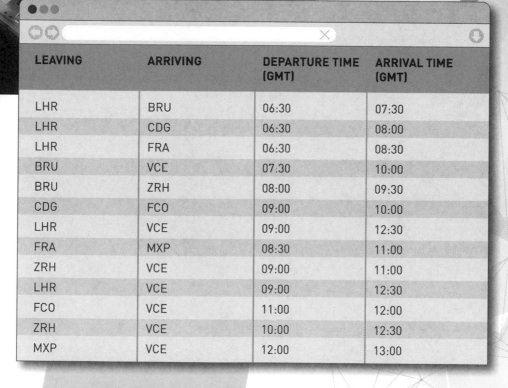

LEAVING	ARRIVING	DEPARTURE TIME (GMT)	ARRIVAL TIME (GMT)
LHR	BRU	06:30	07:30
LHR	CDG	06:30	08:00
LHR	FRA	06:30	08:30
BRU	VCE	07:30	10:00
BRU	ZRH	08:00	09:30
CDG	FCO	09:00	10:00
LHR	VCE	09:00	12:30
FRA	MXP	08:30	11:00
ZRH	VCE	09:00	11:00
LHR	VCE	09:00	12:30
FCO	VCE	11:00	12:00
ZRH	VCE	10:00	12:30
MXP	VCE	12:00	13:00

stepped out almost directly into the square. It was a place I had never visited in real life, and yet I seemed to know it so well. There had been changes, modernization, of course, but the scale and positioning of things, as well as the well-maintained buildings, gave me a familiarity that was bewildering.

"Quickly! We have no time to waste," instructed Colm, and I followed him to the entrance. "I've called ahead. Getting in shouldn't be the problem it once was for you."

He was right. The two people manning the ticket office waved us through upon seeing us. *This is what it's like being part of a global brotherhood*, I thought. Both of us knew where the secret entrance was; Colm must have seen my simulation clearly. We headed straight there and moved the bricks, which were still hidden behind a tapestry, until the Isu chamber opened up, still humming with power and illumination hundreds of years later.

I moved to the final panel, which was still glowing from when Vejovis had lit it up, and continued further into the Isu stronghold. I noticed that further parts of the room had changed, giving me a lot more to work on, but as I approached the back part of the room, a small alcove drew back to allow me entry, just from my presence. I was confused but relieved.

The inside revealed what looked like an electrical control panel with wires of different shapes spanning the sides. They seemed to link up to one another but weren't all facing in the correct directions to complete a circuit. I realized that I could spin individual blocks in any direction, any angle. Two of the side pieces seemed to have connections. Perhaps I had to link those parts, but which blocks did I need to spin?

"Nice work," Colm confirmed as we were rushing to the departure gate, checking my route on his phone. "Keep your head down on the plane. They may have already got someone else on this flight."

I normally enjoyed flying but the inability to have any effect on our journey was frustrating. Perhaps I should have sat back and enjoyed being forced to relax for a moment too. Colm ate a surprisingly generous in-flight meal – probably the smart move – but I sat quietly and still. I tried to keep an eye on the other transfers to note who else may be taking the same route but didn't notice anyone doing what we were doing. Colm seemed confident and positive, although I knew we still had a lot to do before the blade was in our hands.

After our speedy transfers, we touched down in Venice Marco Polo Airport and hopped into a taxi that would take us off the mainland and to St Mark's Basilica. Colm's Italian was impressive. He was clearly more of a man of the world than I realized, although I seemed to understand a lot more than I had expected to; perhaps a symptom of the Bleeding Effect again.

Our taxi arrived at the Basilica and we

On the opposite side was a list of lines with letters next to them. Next to the letters, the words "Only use wire numbers – Only use climbing colours" were written. It confused me at first but I guessed that whatever answer I got from the wires would be the only lines I needed.

FOR **DIFFICULT** HINTS, TURN TO PAGE **163**

FOR **MEDIUM** HINTS, TURN TO PAGE **173**

FOR **EASY** HINTS, TURN TO PAGE **183**

FOR **SOLUTIONS**, TURN TO PAGE **201**

In the middle of the room, there was another wall. My excitement was dulled by frustration. When I looked back at Colm, he seemed unimpressed, until a gentle whirring increased in volume and pitch, taking with it the second back wall of the chamber. Memories of it flashed around my head, throwing me to the floor... except I had never seen this. These could not have been my memories.

Colm came to my aid, picking me up and holding me in front of the deep cavern that had opened up. My head was pulsing but I could see into the cavern and it seemed to go on forever. Cuboids jutted out from each other in what seemed like a random order but was more likely just a design beyond my own understanding.

I squinted into the darkness. We both looked back up to see what appeared to be a

spotlight illuminating a metallic object in a case. It was the blade.

"Do you have the other half?" I asked Colm.

His eyes widened in wonder as he looked over at me, smiled and nodded. His smile grew to something a lot more menacing and he suddenly released his hold on me. Another nod was followed by a sharp kick to my chest as Colm knocked me off the edge of the chasm, plunging me into the darkness below.

I flailed around, desperately grasping for something to cling on to and, after what seemed like minutes of falling in slow motion, my right hand touched something solid. I spun around to put my other hand out, scraping down the sides of the chasm, until a block jutting from the wall caught some of my momentum. I couldn't hold on but it slowed me enough to gather my senses and spot another nearby wall that I may be able to

141

cling to. I pushed up and away from the wall, which didn't stop me, but slowed me again, and launched me to the other side. I landed and hung on to the wall for dear life. Tens of meters below the ground now, I was alive and able to gather myself. I alternated hands for a few seconds, to give each one time to rest, and looked up to see Colm holding a torch above me, unaware that I could possibly be alive. My only option now was to climb.

I looked up to see three different colours of handholds. The one I was holding onto – green – didn't move. Every few seconds, the others would move in or out. While they were in, I couldn't use them. I figured out I could move over two handholds of a set colour before they shifted and I could probably time it just right to shift between the colours as they were changing. I could wait as long as I liked on any handhold while it was out. Strangely, there were panels between some of the handholds in unusual colours, but I realized I would only pass some of them. I had to make it up to the top.

FOR **DIFFICULT** HINTS, TURN TO PAGE **163**
FOR **MEDIUM** HINTS, TURN TO PAGE **173**
FOR **EASY** HINTS, TURN TO PAGE **183**
FOR **SOLUTIONS**, TURN TO PAGE **202**

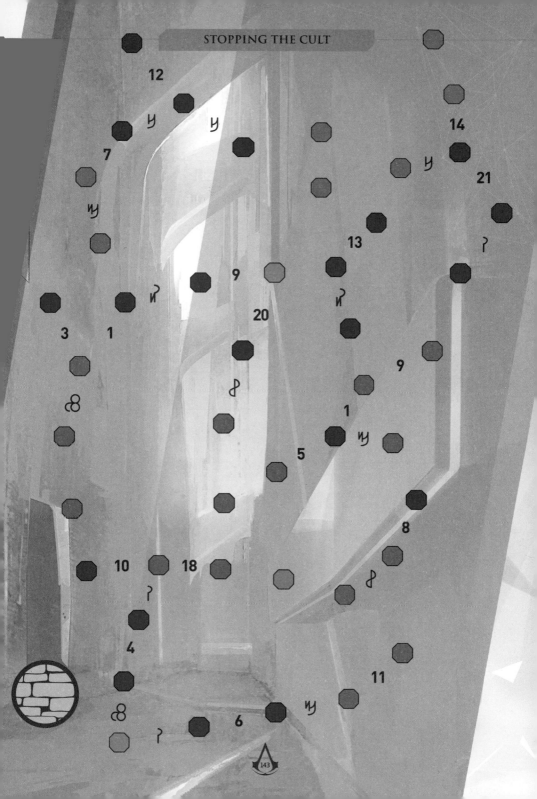

When I got closer to the top, I couldn't see Colm anywhere. I couldn't believe he had betrayed me. I thought back over the earlier conversation with Alera and realized that she wasn't admitting to being a Templar but, instead, assumed I was. In the end, it was Colm that must have called them in. That's why he was so eager to get here and outrun her. I found my breath and climbed further up, hoping to gain some kind of advantage over him and find where he was. I reached an outcrop that spanned the cavern and

hauled myself on to the platform, which was surrounded by thin, metallic struts. Colm was ahead but below me, heading toward the illuminated podium with the blade. I had not only found it, but led the Templars right to it. I hurried over to a position above Colm that would allow me to put an end to him. Looking down, I saw symbols on the floor that I hadn't noticed from ground level. Colm was still standing there, the case seemingly locked. He kicked it in frustration, perhaps realizing that he should not have betrayed me quite yet. He

looked around, hoping for an easy solution, then something told him to raise his head, but I had already started falling toward him, my arm held backward, clasping one of the struts that I had snapped off my walkway.

Time seemed to slow down as we both contemplated the inevitability of what was about to happen. He started to move out of the way but I knew he couldn't reach safety. I could see where his arms were moving and would easily be able to adjust my own to avoid him batting my hand out of the way. He was

done. And then it hit me.

A flash of the past, or the future, or nothing real at all, confusing me and ruining my concentration. I was on the floor, the makeshift blade lying close to Colm, who had managed to block me in my dazed state. He was hurt from the power of my fall but climbed to his feet before me and kicked my piece of metal off the side. I was defenceless and he had one half of the blade.

A clunk from the entrance took his attention. That was my chance. I jumped

to my feet and charged Colm, grabbing his blade hand to stop him from using it on me. He was stronger than me, so I clasped my second hand to his and managed to keep the blade from my chest. He balled his other hand into a fist and smashed it into my ribs, weakening my grip, and grabbed my closest wrist. Putting all his power into it, he threw me away and I landed on the floor close to the pedestal with the blade in it. I looked quickly to see if I could open it and arm myself, but it was closed.

"Already tried, I'm afraid," he said, spitting the words at me with disgust. "I'll tell you what: if you open it for me, I won't kill you."

I looked back at it and saw a 4x4 keypad underneath the blade. I was not going to overpower him and, even if I opened the lock, I had lost my element of surprise. My head throbbed with visions of the past again.

"Are you still in there, Joey?" Colm said with a chuckle.

He was far better trained than me, physically stronger and, despite the skills I'd learned from my experiences in the Animus, I couldn't harness them properly without losing myself in these visions.

"The Bleeding Effect looks pretty nasty," he continued.

I just had to concentrate on the keypad. Everything I had seen inside this Isu structure would lead me to the code. That was why I was here. But how would I get out of this? I picked myself up, walked over to the pad and thought for a moment.

! SOLVE TO PASS

When I knew which location the Animus was pointing me toward, I knew I could proceed.

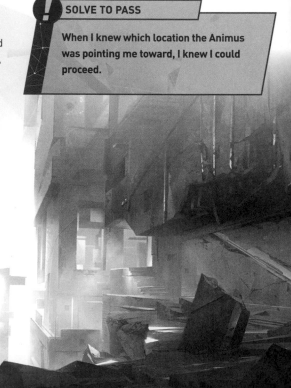

O

F

V

C

N L U E

D I A P

O S T R

B C A M

Z R H D

FOR **DIFFICULT** HINTS, TURN TO PAGE **163**
FOR **MEDIUM** HINTS, TURN TO PAGE **173**
FOR **EASY** HINTS, TURN TO PAGE **183**
FOR **SOLUTIONS**, TURN TO PAGE **203**

I tapped the code into the keypad and, almost immediately, the glass started rising, but not fast enough for me to grab the blade before Colm could get to me. I span around and tried to keep eye contact with him.

"Move away from it," he ordered.

I was happy to comply, walking in the opposite direction to him so he wouldn't turn around. A few seconds was long enough.

"Hey, Colm," I chirped confidently.

"What?"

"I see now why you were so insistent we got here so fast."

"Oh yeah? And why's that?"

"What do you think that 'clunk' was earlier?"

And on that, Alera's blade pierced straight through the front of Colm's neck. He looked up at me in shock, then fear, then nothing. He collapsed to the floor. Colm was dead. I half-expected the world to fade around me so that he could appear in front of me chewing the scenery about how little I understood, or how right he was, but this was no simulation.

"Joey, are you OK?" Alera asked.

"Yeah, I think so."

"My apologies for earlier. I've known Colm for years. I didn't suspect it was him that had brought the Templars to us."

"That's OK," I said, smiling. "It's all worked out."

Alera looked over at the blade, on the now fully open pedestal, and then down to the one in Colm's hand. She crouched, picked it up and threw it over to me. I snatched it out of the air without a shadow of doubt. How far I had come in my brief time with the Assassins.

"You'd better put the blades together," Alera suggested.

I nodded and walked over to the other blade. It looked so small and, since I had one that looked just like it, it seemed so irrelevant, but

I could feel the power as I moved my hands closer. I touched the flat edge of the blade and took a deep breath. This was it. Picking up the second blade, it was easy – almost magnetic – to bring them together and, when I did, the entire double-bladed weapon erupted in a bright glow. It seemed as though my mind was playing tricks with me. I didn't understand what was happening. I shut my eyes against the glow and, when I opened them again, I saw Alera looking down at me in fear.

"Joey? Are you OK?"

I had collapsed. For how long I didn't know.

"The Bleeding Effect. It's gone too far," she continued.

"What do I do? How do I stop it?" I pleaded.

"We have to create a Synch Nexus," she announced confidently.

"What on earth is that?"

"We've been pulling you out of your experiences too fast. When you're in the Animus and you don't experience a whole memory, you don't fully synchronize with it. It's led to this."

"Don't fully synchronize...?" I stuttered, confused.

"Yes. There are things you haven't considered. Things that were important to these people, that they have showed you, yet you haven't used. If you can achieve full synchronization, there is a chance this could stop."

My mind erupted in images. Images from the past that seemed familiar. Of course, the images I saw in this chamber from above were in some way tied to different elements from my times in the Animus. If I could use these symbols and these specific elements from my adventures in the past, it may help me fully synchronize. It may allow me to achieve a Synch Nexus. I concentrated on it all and sought out things I had not used. Once I had done all of this, it would help me learn something about myself; about who I really was.

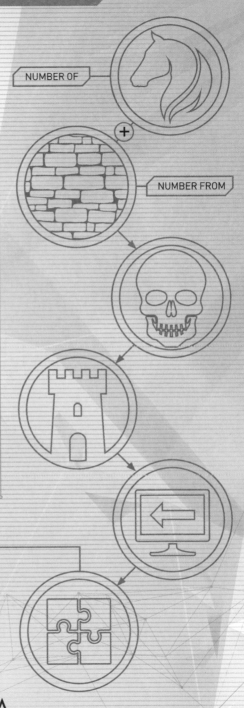

NUMBER OF

NUMBER FROM

! SOLVE TO PASS

Once I knew my true identity, I knew I could proceed.

Vejovis? How could I be Vejovis? I spoke the name and a huge holographic projection came to life in the room above a circular platform. It was him.

"Joey, it is a pleasure to finally meet you in the flesh."

"You're real?" I replied.

"I will be corporeal before long."

"Your whole plan was to live again. You want to become Malcolm? You want to become The Connection?"

"Thanks to you. You have brought the blades together and now the power of the Piece of Eden is complete. You have put the wheels in motion to bring about my resurrection."

Alera lunged at the hologram but fell straight through and onto the floor. Vejovis, without a second thought, swiped at her and she flew into the wall behind her, the impact

knocking her out.

"Leave her alone."

"Do you not realize? It was you that did that." He chuckled.

I looked down at my hands. They were stinging.

"You made me do that."

"In a sense. You are me. An incarnation of me. A Sage."

"I don't understand."

"All of the people you have seen through the eyes of. They were all Sages. My Sages. And by connecting them all, you have taken all of those portions of me and brought them together. The Bleeding Effect has given you every part of me. Don't you see, Joey? *You* are The Connection."

My world sank. Everything I had been doing was for someone else. Someone who just wanted to control and enslave.

"All this time," he continued, "these pieces have been waiting to come back together. You have connected my Sages. Now you have connected the blades. Next, you and I will become fully connected as my being bleeds into yours."

"This can't be."

"It can. And those flashes you are experiencing are signs that the moment is closer."

I paused for a second. The flashes had stopped. By completing my memories, I had created a Synch Nexus. I could make my mind my own. But even in this moment of clarity, Vejovis was growing more powerful. If all my actions up to this point and all my objectives had been in service of this Isu being, there was one action I could take that would stop him in his tracks.

I had to split the blades, and I was still holding them. I put the weapon on the floor and lifted one edge, stamping in the middle to separate them into two. The blades were already held together so strongly that it didn't simply separate the two pieces, but shattered the bottom piece into multiple fragments, which scattered across the floor and bounced down the sides of the chasm, erupting into glowing sparks. Vejovis looked horrified.

"What are you doing?" he screamed.

"Disconnecting you," I quipped, plunging the remaining blade into the platform that I assumed he was emanating from.

His hologram glitched out of existence and I was left in silence for a few moments.

"Disconnecting you?" came Alera's voice from across the room.

She had woken up just in time to hear my best attempt at a smart Hollywood one-liner.

"Look, it's not like I had much time to think."

"Oh, I liked it. The Connection. A digital being... 'disconnecting' works."

I smiled.

"So what do you think happened to Vejovis?" I asked. "Did I kill him?"

"Honestly, I don't know. From what we've seen, the Isu that have survived somehow do so in a way that we don't understand. You've broken the blade."

"Sorry. I knew the Assassins wanted it."

"We just didn't want it to fall into the Templars' hands," Alera reassured. "And by doing that, you've stopped Malcolm existing, as in your vision."

"I don't get it. What was that vision?"

"Something Vejovis planted in your mind, hoping for it to be a self-fulfilling prophecy. I guess he underestimated you."

"When this started, I couldn't have done this. He caused me to become someone that could defeat him."

"My point stands," Alera said, smiling.

"So what now?" I asked.

"Imminent danger minimal. Perhaps we should get out of here in case the rest of the Templars show up."

I nodded, clutching the remaining blade to my chest, and followed Alera back to the entrance. As we tried to close the paths that had taken us to where we had ended up, I thought about Vejovis and how we had stopped him. The holographic projection had just been a manifestation – like a simulation of him – and destroying whatever was projecting him would not actually destroy *him*. He remained hidden and distributed around whatever Isu network had been hosting them all. For now.

I felt like I had seen inside that network somehow and had been left with its name: the "Grey". And it wasn't just Isu inside. I had been there briefly but did not want to return.

As I emerged into the Basilica itself and regained signal on my mobile phone, a chatter of messages came in. They were from my boss at the museum.

"Where are you?" "What happened?" "I can't keep you on after all this. I'm sorry. You're fired."

I smiled. There was more to the world than I had ever imagined before, with places and times to go that I could not have hoped for in my previous life.

Alera looked up at me as we stepped into the Venetian sunlight.

"I don't suppose you're looking for a job?"

I smiled at her and nodded.

HINTS

DIFFICULT

PROLOGUE

7

The dots were probably added to assist anyone who did not share the designer's language.

15

Read from left to right but start at the bottom.

CHAPTER ONE

THE ANIMUS

21

Judge the distances carefully.

27

If I look around, I'll find more than a needle in the haystack.

31

How do I find the 'perfect combination'?

35

My target looks like someone who has others to run his errands for him.

CHAPTER TWO

TRAINING

47

Each symbol correlates with the letter and number preceding it.

49

The answer relates back to the previous puzzle.

53

I will not need to visit all nine rooftops.

55

Starting with the croc with the strange markings, follow the direction that the next crocodile is pointing.

57

The crocodiles have the key.

58

Remember my rooftop jaunt?

CHAPTER THREE

FOLLOWING THE TRAIL

67

My destination is not on the map.

69

Does this look familiar? Maybe I should review my earlier adventures.

75

This looks like a process of elimination using the most recent clues.

CHAPTER FOUR

DECEIVING
THE ASSASINS

89

Navigate through the shadows.

92-93

There is one vulnerability in this network.

94-95

Things will become clearer after I ascend.

97

My jumping distance hasn't improved since my last climbing
adventure.

98-99

Do these colours look familiar?

100

Those symbols relate to my recent adventures somehow.

103

I need to order my scattered thoughts into a coherent shape.

CHAPTER FIVE

A HIDDEN TOMB

118

This map masks its true purpose.

120

Where have I seen those shapes before?

123

I can leap over the white-garbed ones, they do not count.

126

The thing that is hidden in the room will only be revealed by searching.

129

The inputs are out there.

CHAPTER SIX

STOPPING THE CULT

137

The direct route is not the fastest.

139

Connecting flight, connecting wires ... it's all connected.

143

If I still need a hint on how to climb a wall, maybe I'm not Assassin material!

147

I need to coordinate these coordinates.

149

I will need to review my adventures from the moment I joined the Assassins.

HINTS

MEDIUM

PROLOGUE

7

I know an anagram when I see one!

11

The name is comprised of just three letters.

CHAPTER ONE

THE ANIMUS

21

At some point I might need to go down to reach the top.

27

I learned something when I overcame my fear of heights.

31

When carrying cash, take the largest denominations possible.

35

His wool accessories are an obvious attempt to blend in with the crowd.

CHAPTER TWO

TRAINING

47

The numbers and letters could be coordinates.

49

The symbols in the equations belong to a sequence of natural numbers. Which of the five equations holds the key to solving the others?

53

Make a note of which hieroglyphics I land on, in the order that I land on them.

55

You should never smile at a crocodile but maybe follow their noses ...

57

The functions will make sense at the door.

58

The numbers are probably a substitution code.

CHAPTER THREE

FOLLOWING THE TRAIL

67

Maybe if I join the dots ...

69

Not everything is straightforward.

75

Each of these yields two words: the wheel within a wheel, the Viking seer stones and the bell tower.

CHAPTER FOUR

DECEIVING THE ASSASINS

89

Every move I make must be unobserved. Keep track of my direction of travel.

92-93

Make connections to find the fault.

94-95

I should keep my eyes open for these colours.

97

Remember that I'll need to rest after four jumps and after jumping from a crack – and I can only do that once!

98-99

The three colours form three distinct shapes within the grid.

100

I'm going to need to retrace and reapply my steps to make the equation add up.

103

Why does the prospect of imminent death bring to mind a Chinese puzzle?

CHAPTER FIVE

A HIDDEN TOMB

118

I should keep an eye out for these colours as I explore Venice.

120

The colours are familiar, and I feel the number of feathers is important.

123

There are numbers in this crowd.

126

There is something in the route. Follow the lines.

129

There are three symbols, each with a four-digit input.

CHAPTER SIX

STOPPING THE CULT

137

Looks like my favourite Renaissance inventor could help me out here!

139

Rotate five squares to complete the circuit.

143

Do I need a hint? Climbing should be second nature to me now!

147

I hope I didn't get my wires crossed earlier.

149

I have seen these symbols twice during my journey. There's a relationship between numbers, colours, symbols and letters.

HINTS

EASY

PROLOGUE

6

The dots run from 1 to 6, put them into order, then read the letters in that order.

10

The direction that the men are pointing depends on the colour of their shirt and determined by the compass tattoo.

CHAPTER ONE

THE ANIMUS

21

Only count the letters on the *lines* that connect the handholds.

27

One from the tower and one from the maze. The third could be compiled with a pitchfork.

31

Where have I seen these numbers and letters recently?

35

Check the boss's supplies list and the key combination.

CHAPTER TWO

TRAINING

47

Could each symbol represent a map location?

49

This equation should make things clearer.

$$Ɑ \times Ɑ = Ɑ$$

53

I should work out which pages are duplicated before starting my journey across the rooftops.

55

If each crocodile is pointing at another, I feel I can decern a shape, mayabe a number?

57

Cross-reference the glyphs with the crocodile key in the order that the guards were dispatched.

58

Modify the numbers using the functions I got after eliminating the guards.

CHAPTER THREE

FOLLOWING THE TRAIL

67

The first route from Yerevan to Dammam, looks rather like a letter.

69

The letters are jumbled up and make two words when unscrambled.

75

What do I know about 'Oilmaker'? What two things did I learn from climbing? I can learn two more by turning the inner wheel, guided by the parchment. Look to the runes for a name and a place. The threads will make everything clearer.

CHAPTER FOUR
DECEIVING THE ASSASINS

89

Make a note of the compass directions as I move from one point to the next. I must avoid the gaze of the guards, which extends *beyond* the yellow cone.

92-93

Join up all the numbers that are within the army's travelling distance. To get from Masyaf to Damascus, there is one number that *must* be visited.

94-95

I think some of these dots need to be joined, but which ones? Perhaps the city holds a clue …

97

Look ahead for that single crack/rest combo. Don't forget to keep track of the numbers that I jump over.

98-99

Maybe I can apply the patterns formed by the three colours to the markings on the reverse of the map?

100

Did I remember to count each move I made when sneaking into the village? Could these numbers correlate with my recent climbing adventure?

103

If I can square this unfortunate situation, I think I can get on top of things.

CHAPTER FIVE

A HIDDEN TOMB

118

The distinctive shape of each canal is significant. I may need to refer to this map later.

120

The colour of a mask and the number of feathers on each side are somehow connected to the canal map. How do I find two letters for each mask?

123

Look for four distinct shapes as I make my way through the throng.

126

Vejovis has just told me the route. There are shapes within it, could they be numbers?

129

A simple substitution cypher, but I'll need to know which numbers to input. I've seen these symbols before.

CHAPTER SIX

STOPPING
THE CULT

137

My route will take me from London to Italy via France.

139

Could those letters be airport codes?

143

Note any numbers and symbols that I pass over.

147

If I check the coordinates from left to right in the wires puzzle and apply them to the keypad, all will become clear.

149

If I apply the number of horses to each of the numbers collected on my last climb and figure out what the symbols mean, I'm sure I can crack the code.

SOLUTIONS

PROLOGUE

6-7

1	2	3	4	5	6
O	P	E	N	M	E

10-11

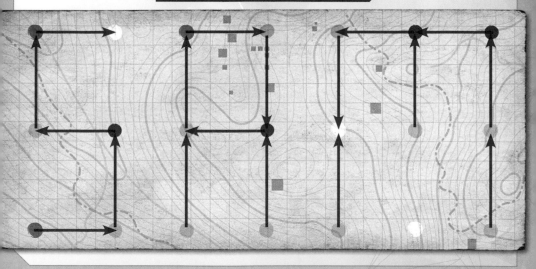

CHAPTER ONE

THE ANIMUS

26-27

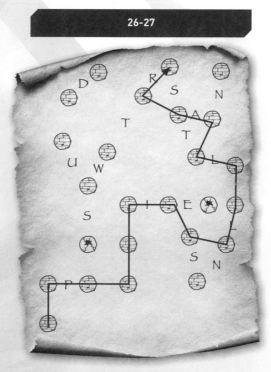

The word is PILLAR.

20-21

The PILLAR is from the tower on page 25.
The SWORD is obtained from the maze on page 29.
The six letters from the haystack make the word DAGGER.

31

Wool necklace	13d	2o
Wool bracelet	20d	5o
Sandals	20d	2o
Blue tunic	46d	1o

The code is: 1m 20d 4o

34-35

Having worked out the supplies from the list on page
28, I know that the boss has a blue tunic.

CHAPTER TWO
TRAINING

47

Cross-referencing the numbers and letters on the map grid highlights the following locations:

4	G	GREECE
8	I	GEORGIA
8	E	SYRIA
6	A	EGYPT
4	D	MEDITERRANEAN

49

$$5 + 3 = 4 + 4$$
$$3 \times 3 = 4 + 5$$
$$1 + 1 = 2$$
$$4 \times 1 = 4$$
$$1 + 2 = 3$$

The fourth equation holds the key, since we know that one of the glyphs must equal 1 (as x multiplied by x is x). The symbol representing the number 4 relates to the coordinates 6A on the map, which leads to Egypt.

53

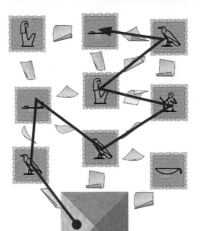

55

Tracing the gazes of the five crocodiles creates the number '6'.

57

Cross-referencing the number '6' with the glyphs in the correct sequence provides the following functions:

+6   -4   x1   +5   +1   ÷2   +3

58

Translating the hieroglyphics from the rooftops gives me:

2   5   2   4   1   2   5

Find the functions by cross-referencing the temple hieroglyphics with the '6' column. Then apply the functions ...

+6   -4   x1   +5   +1   ÷2   +3

8   1   2   9   2   1   8

... and put the resultant numbers through a simple substitution cypher (A =1, B=2, etc).

H   A   B   I   B   A   H

CHAPTER THREE

FOLLOWING THE TRAIL

67

Each of the six journeys forms a letter: LONDON.

69

The letters are E, A, V, R, J, E, I, S, D, D, T.

75

First, I should look at the threads to see if anything is missing. If 'Oilmaker' doesn't have one or two guards and the 'Connection' has four guards, then 'Oilmaker' must have five guards and also have a limp, which means his name isn't David or Stowe.

From the climbing puzzle I can unscramble two pertinent words: David and Jester. If David is 'Jester' then he has two guards, is located in Wycham and has Golden Robes.

I made a copy of the wheel on page 77, cut it out and placed it inside the wheel on page 73. Following the instructions on the parchment, I turned the inner wheel so that the first two letters were lined up. Then I checked the letter that aligned with the third.

If K is B, then F is V

If U is B, then V is O

If C is J, then L is Y

If S is Z, then W is A

If F is V, then W is G

If S is A, then L is E

If C is G, then T is U

If E is P, then K is R

If O is L, then J is E

If E is B, then I is D

If H is G, then R is W

If U is X, then H is A

If M is P, then Y is R

If S is N, then Q is D

This tells me that Edward is 'Voyager' and therefore has a pet wolf.

The **Runes** can be ordered into two pertinent words: RHODRI and LUNDEN

I know that Stowe is located at Jorvik, so Edward must be located in Essexe and therefore have one Guard. As 'Oilmaker' is not Stowe, he must be Rhodri, which means Stowe is 'Connection', has four guards and an eyepatch.

NAME	IDENTIFIER	LOCATION	NICKNAME	GUARDS
Rhodri	Limp	Lunden	Oilmaker	Five Guards
David	Golden Robes	Wycham	Jester	Two Guards
Edward	Pet Wolf	Essexe	Voyager	One Guard
Stone	Eyepatch	Jorvik	Connection	Four Guards

81

Using the information that I gathered about the 'Connection' from the previous puzzle...

My name – 1. The first letter of Stowe is S.

My identifier – 2. The second letter of Eyepatch is Y.

My Location – 3. The third letter of Jorvik is R.

My nickname – 8. The eighth letter of Connection is I.

My number of guards – 7. The seventh letter of Four Guards is A.

The answer is Syria.

CHAPTER FOUR

DECEIVING THE ASSASINS

89

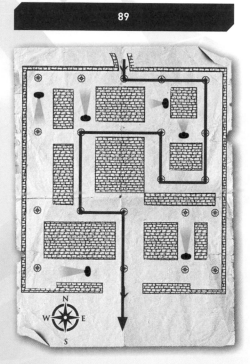

I reached the entrance in eleven moves, travelling as follows:
1 E, 2 E, 3 S, 4 S, 5 W, 6 N, 7 W, 8 S, 9 E, 10 S, 11 S

92-93

Pot number 9 is the one I must sabotage.

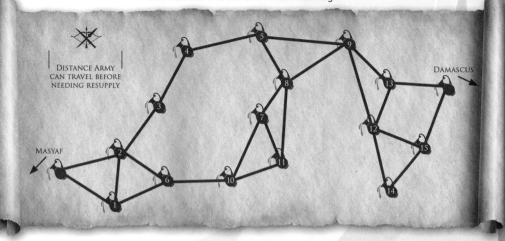

DISTANCE ARMY CAN TRAVEL BEFORE NEEDING RESUPPLY

MASYAF

DAMASCUS

94-95

The glitch on page 98 created patterns which can be applied to the matching-coloured dots like so...

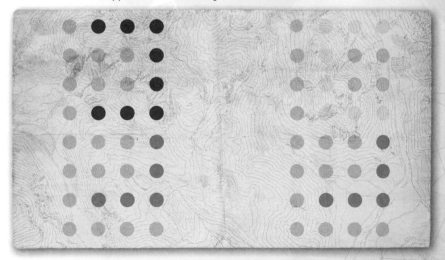

I can now see the number 35.

My route takes me through the numbers 6, 5, 3, 9 and 11.

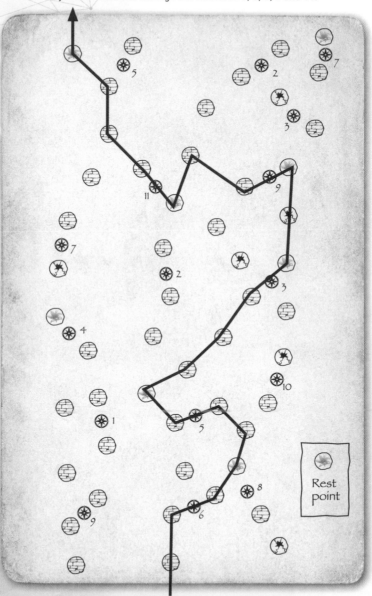

98-99

The glitch creates the following colour shapes:

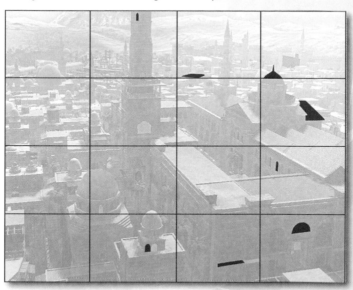

100

The answer is 206. The Jug puzzle solution (9) multiplied by the dots (35) minus 9, which is the number obtained from applying the climbing numbers 6 5 3 9 11 to the stealth puzzle solution 1 E, 2 E, 3 S, 4 S, 5 W, 6 N, 7 W, 8 S, 9 E, 10 S, 11 S. This gives me N, W, S, E and S. If I draw five lines that follow these directions, I get a figure 9.

103

Arrange the shapes into a square as shown. I will need to cut the rope and drop the crate to eliminate Rafee.

CHAPTER FIVE

A HIDDEN TOMB

118

The canal shapes and the colour sequence are connected to the mask puzzle on page 120.

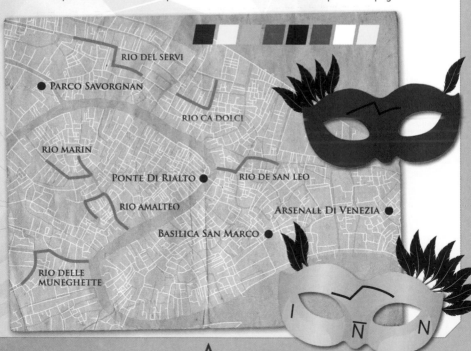

Each canal on the map has a distinctive shape which matches the shape on
one of the masks.
Each mask has a number of feathers on its left and right side. These numbers
relate to letters in the corresponding canal name.
Combining the two letters creates a symbol which will serve as a key for the
puzzle on the page given. Position Da Vinci's machine so that two symbols
and a letter are visible through the holes. Make a note of the letter.

Mask	Canal	Feathers	Letters	Key	Puzzle	Solution		
Yellow	Rio de San Leo	2	8	I	N	IN	p.120	A
Red	Rio del Servi	5	1	E	R	ER	p.125	B
Blue	Rio Marin	4	5	M	A	MA	p.131	I
Green	Rio Ca Dolci	6	3	D	O	DO	p.132	S
White	Rio Delle Muneghette	5	6	E	L	EL	p.127	C
Black	Rio Amalteo	8	7	T	L	TL	p.139	L

By arranging the letters in the colour order from the canal map, I get:

B A S I L I C A

Basilica.

The repeated colour sequence is Yellow – Red – Yellow – Blue – Blue – Green
which you can see on [page 121]
Tracing the route, which is broken by the white figures, reveals the numbers **5 7 2 7**.

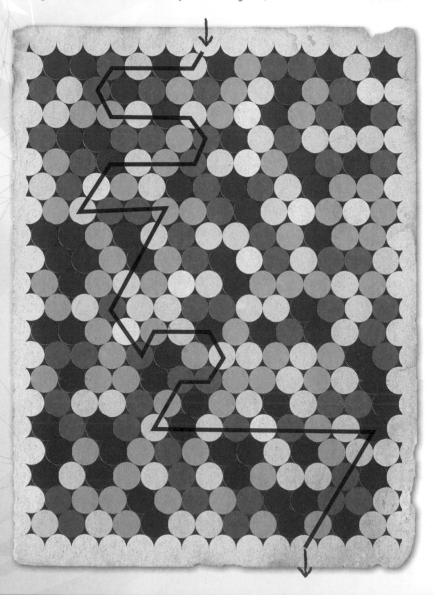

126

The route is: Down 3, Right 1, Up 1, Left 2, Down 2, Left 5, Down 2, Right 3, Up 6. Following this route, you can see the numbers **8 9 3 6**.

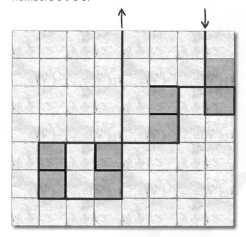

127

The numbers are **4 3 8 2**.

129

The Assassination puzzle (page 126) provided the numbers **8 9 3 6**. The Crowd (page 123) gave the numbers **5 7 2 7** and the Secret Entrance (page 127) revealed **4 3 8 2**. When I plug these numbers into the hologram, I get 10, 15, 5, 25. If 3 is 'C', I can infer that 10 = J, 15 = O, 5 = E and 25 = Y. Hey, it's my name!

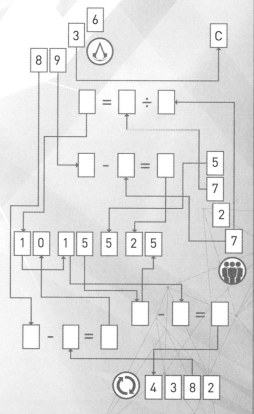

CHAPTER SIX

STOPPING THE CULT

137

The fastest route from London Heathrow (**LHR**) is the 06.30 flight to Paris Charles de Gaulle (**CDG**) which arrives at 08.00. Then I take the 09.00 flight to Rome–Fiumicino International Airport (**FCO**) - also known as 'Leonardo da Vinci' Airport- and from there take the 11.00 flight to Venice Marco Polo (**VCE**) which arrives at 12.00, half an hour earlier than the direct flight from London!

LEAVING	ARRIVING	DEPARTURE TIME (GMT)	ARRIVAL TIME (GMT)
LHR	BRU	06:30	07:30
LHR	CDG	06:30	08:00
LHR	FRA	06:30	08:30
BRU	VCE	07:30	10:00
BRU	ZRH	08:00	09:30
CDG	FCO	09:00	10:00
LHR	VCE	09:00	12:30
FRA	MXP	08:30	11:00
ZRH	VCE	09:00	11:00
LHR	VCE	09:00	12:30
FCO	VCE	11:00	12:00
ZRH	VCE	10:00	12:30
MXP	VCE	12:00	13:00

I filled in the missing letters from the connecting flights: CDG
and FCO. The circuit is completed by rotating the squares at the
following coordinates: FH, OR, OD, VD, CH.

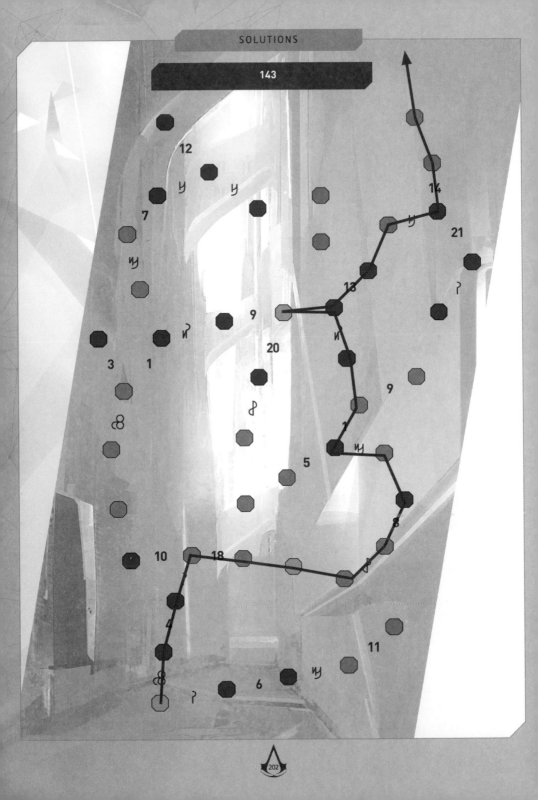

143

147

Using the coordinates obtained from the puzzle on page
139 and cross-referencing them in this puzzle I get ...

FH = A
OR = L
OD = E
VD = R
CH = A

149

Start with the numbers obtained from my last wall climbing adventure. To each number add the
number of horses (4) on page 121. Make a note of the symbols that connect with the climbing
numbers, they match up with the symbols on the bodies from page 76.

Wall numbers	4	18	8	1	13	14
+4	8	22	12	5	17	18
Symbols	৪	?	৪	ꭹ	ꭎ	ꭹ
Bodies	Red	Green	Magenta	Blue	Yellow	Orange

The tower on page 20 arranges the colours like so:

Magneta (12)		Red (8)	
Yellow (17)	Blue (5)		Orange (18)
Green (22)		Blue (5)	

Following the arrows from the screen on page 49, gives me the order in which these should be read.

Blue	Green	Yellow	Magenta	Blue	Orange	Red
5	22	17	12	5	18	8

The tangram on page 108 provides the final clue. It's a letter-number substitution cypher. If Z=1 and
Y=2, I can conclude that:

5	22	17	12	5	18	8
V	E	J	O	V	I	S